POEMS TALKING TO POEMS

POEMS TALKING TO POEMS

Setting Your Poetry Manuscript Apart

Edited by Jeffrey Levine and Kristina Marie Darling

Tupelo Press
North Adams, Massachusetts

Poems Talking to Poems: Setting Your Poetry Manuscript Apart

Edited by Jeffrey Levine and Kristina Marie Darling

Library of Congress Cataloging-in-Publication data available upon request.

ISBN-13: 978-1-961209-36-7 (paperback)
978-1-961209-47-3 (ebook)

Cover and text design by Allison O'Keefe

Cover image: Alexander Calder, "France Forever," 1942, © 2025 Calder Foundation, New York / Artists Rights Society (ARS), New York.

Photo courtesy of Calder Foundation, New York / Art Resource, New York.

First paperback edition October 2025

Tupelo Press
P.O. Box 1767
North Adams, Massachusetts 01247
(413) 664-9611 / Fax: (413) 664-9711 editor@tupelopress.org /
www.tupelopress.org

Tupelo Press is an award-winning independent literary press that publishes fine fiction, non- fiction, and poetry in books that are a joy to hold as well as read. Tupelo Press is a registered 501(c)(3) nonprofit organization, and we rely on public support to carry out our mission of publishing extraordinary work that may be outside the realm of the large commercial publishers. Financial donations are welcome and are tax deductible.

Contents

The Poetry Manuscript: Arts and Crafts

Jeffrey Levine

This essay is adapted from the "On Making the Poetry Manuscript" series, originally published on Jeffrey Levine's blog (jeffreylevine.com) from October 2011 to September 2014. Jeffrey Levine is the founder, Publisher, and Artistic Director of Tupelo Press.

The following tips on how to form a book from a stack of individual poems have accumulated thousands of views since the first post in 2011. Now, more than a decade and hundreds of poetry manuscript conferences later, these tips remain tried and true, and comprise a rubric for the poets and Tupelo authors I mentor. Some of the following advice remains concrete, generic, and "merely" stylistic, although even nuts and bolts have some intrinsic value when collected in one place. As style is a matter of taste, you must consider that what I say reflects my own prejudices and preferences.

Most of my advice concerns more artistic matters: What is the artistic process as applied to making a poetry manuscript cohere? What are some useful approaches to the art of transforming individual poems into a transcendent whole?

The Art of the Manuscript

1) When organizing the manuscript, your aim is to create nothing less than a work of art. As Robert Frost famously suggested (in so many words), if there are 27 poems in a book, the book itself is the final poem. You'll want to think about what your book is "about," and to include poems that carry those themes, that are somehow related, that "speak" to each other. It's also a good idea to tether poems together that are written

more or less in the same creative period, lest they sound as though written by different poets—different versions of you. I don't mean to suggest that a book needs to be written in any particular timeframe, but rather that the book should include poems written during a period (a year, two years, five years, whatever) when your creative strategies have been consistent.

2) Every time we write a poem, we announce to the world what we think a poem is. The poems you write when urging—wittingly or unconsciously—a particular aesthetic are the ones that belong in the same book. Spread all of your poems out on the floor, a floor that doesn't need to be disturbed (easy for me to say, I know), and look at them. Read them out loud. Live with them for days and days. See what relationships might begin to develop between poems. What does that poem by the bureau have to say to the poem under the bed? Where do you see common images developing? In what directions do your various threads lead? What seem to be your concerns as a poet during this period of creativity, and how do they seem to want to group? What discoveries are your poems making? The process of inclusion and ordering is organic, calculated, thoughtful, instinctual, unconscious, and somewhat Zen. You need time to permit all of those matters and antimatters to work upon you, and upon your poems.

3) When ordering poems in your manuscript, pay no attention to which poems have been published (and where), and which poems have not. At the conclusion of contests, I often (call me perverse) go back and look at the acknowledgment pages of finalists and semifinalists. I find that most poets place an inordinate and mistaken reliance on their publishing history in ordering poems (or in deciding to include certain poems). Many of us assume that because a journal editor smiled on a particular poem it must be better than the poems not taken, or that a poem taken by *Poetry* or *Agni* must be better than one taken by a lesser-known publication. I am almost always amazed—*amazed*—on learning which poems have been taken and which have not, and by whom.

Nothing could be less relevant to creating a manuscript than whether and where the individual poems found a home. If you believe in your poems, and if you have good reason for believing that they belong together in a particular manuscript, then include them, and order them according to your own aesthetic judgment. Period. If your poem published in the *New Yorker* doesn't work in this particular manuscript, save it for another book.

4) Continue to think about each poem according to: mood/tone; dominant images; characters/speaker; setting/season; chronology; and whatever other categories are important to your work. Ask yourself what seem to be the specific concerns addressed in each poem. However you organize your collection, keep in mind that you are creating a book, and you cannot really know how the poems interact with each other unless you've done this work. Make multiple copies of each poem, try different orders with duplicate books, and live with them for a while.

5) Make sure the poems in the beginning of your collection establish the voice and credibility of the manuscript. They should introduce the questions, issues, characters, images, and sources of conflict/tension, etc., that concern you and that will be explored in the book. Think about the trajectory of the manuscript: You want to set the reader off on a journey, a path toward some (even if undisclosed) destination, but unless you're writing an epic, forget about "arc." The notion of "arc" is, in my opinion, too subterranean for any artistic undertaking, except as a result of the felicitous intervention of the muse of artistic balance. First make the book as a whole work; let others praise your "arc."

6) Read your manuscript out loud, to yourself, start to finish. Slowly. Listen attentively. Repeat as needed.

7) Just because a poem has been previously published, or because last Tuesday you decided it was finished, does not mean you can leave

it alone. Rethink, reenter, and if possible, reenvision each poem as if the *Paris Review* hadn't nominated it for a Pushcart Prize. Manuscripts that have achieved semifinalist or finalist status somewhere are perfect candidates for revision. The same thinking applies even after—especially after—your book is taken for publication. Each poem is trying to tell you something you don't already know. Sometimes it takes a poem several years to get through to us. Be attentive. Listen closely. Try things. Try other things.

8) Once you have created an order that feels right, think about dividing the book into separate sections. Ultimately you may or may not elect to go with distinct sections, but this organizational process will encourage you to think even more deeply about your order, about your concerns, and about what makes a poetry book a book. When you see patterns emerging, you might want to go back and think yet again about revision, about new opportunities to open up channels that permit the poems to talk to each other. Yes, it's hard work. We're poets. This is what we do. This is why it's harder than the work of being mortal.

9) Weak poems. You know which ones. Don't "hide" them inside the manuscript. Don't include them. Period.

10) Find an effective title: from the title of a significant poem in your collection, or from a line in one of your poems, or from one of your epigraphs. Try something that may not appear verbatim in your collection at all. But choose a title that somehow signals and amplifies the shape of the manuscript. That said, create about a dozen different titles and live with each for a while. Print out title pages for each possibility, tape them to the refrigerator door, and look at them early and often. Ask someone with cutting-edge aesthetic judgment for their reaction.

Nuts and Bolts

1) Less is more. Keep your manuscript around 48–64 pages maximum. Show your reader you've done the important work of weeding and pruning.

2) Spell-check. Spell-check again.

3) Proofread for consistency of grammar and punctuation. Have a friend do this—someone who can spell and has a deep understanding of grammar rules. It's impossible to proofread your own work, especially a document that's taken years to develop; you "see" what's in your head, not what's on the page.

4) Proofread for the Big Abstractions (i.e., "infinity," "eternity,")—the nineteenth century is over.

5) Proofread for small abstractions (i.e., "dark")—the nineteenth century is still over.

6) Proofread for adverbs (carefully). They're not your friends, unless you're blessed with the lyrical gifts of Seamus Heaney, the word-drunk genius of Albert Goldbarth, or the million-megawatt intelligence and intuition of Anne Carson—in which case, go for it.

7) While we're at it, adjectives are abstractions; earn them well (see above, re Goldbarth, Heaney, and Carson).

8) Proofread for mannerisms (i.e., have you used the word "pale" or "salt" twenty times?).

9) Do you tend to sew up your poems with something willfully plangent ("poetic" with a capital "P") or a Yoda-like dollop of wisdom?

10) Do you tend to begin your poems with a line or two (or an entire stanza) of "throat clearing"?

11) Reread the two preceding questions. Pretend for argument's sake that you've answered yes to both. Now look at each and every poem with fresh eyes and ask yourself: a) Where does each poem really want to start? b) Where does each poem really want to end? Make no mistake: These are deeply artistic matters we're talking about, masquerading as craft questions.

12) When submitting your manuscript, send a cover letter if you like, but not a cv. If you do send a cover letter, make sure it's addressed to the intended press and not to some other press or some other editor (you'd be surprised), and don't address your cover letter to the contest judge (you'd be surprised), and don't say you're in the process of a complete rewrite and will be sending the revised manuscript in a week or two (you'd be surprised), and remember that if it's a contest we're talking about, then no one will read your cover letter, unless you win or come close. If it's an open reading (i.e., not a contest), then publishers love having an opportunity to learn something about the poet. All this said, in reading and selecting manuscripts for publication, it's all about the work, and only about the work.

13) Don't include dedications and thanks in a contest manuscript—there will be plenty of time for that later.

14) Don't title a first book submission "New and Selected."

15) Be judicious about epigraphs—they're hardware unless a poem clearly addresses or plays off of the epigraph in some intrinsic and transformative way.

16) Beware the epigraph that you choose to begin the book with or to announce a new section. Ask yourself whether it's really important

to the poem it sits atop like so much hardware. Do you really want your own language to follow Rilke's or Bishop's?

Rekindling Your Passion for Your Manuscript

How do you turn the rather amorphous parts of my advice on manuscript making (i.e., "include poems that speak to each other") into something more concrete and useful? You've sent your manuscript off into the void dozens of times, maybe you've had the semi-satisfaction of having been a semifinalist a few times, or the nearly heart-wrenching corroborative tease of having been an unrequited finalist. Or perhaps, the void just gobbles up your manuscript over and over again, leaving behind not even a burst of photons.

So there you are again, weary, dispirited, courage at an all-time low, your floor covered with poems, scribbled notes and advice from your best readers on some of them, coffee stains on others, candle wax, a ring or two of red wine, and there they lie in a soup of assorted strategies and typefaces, grumbling at you in a Babel-like cacophony of tongues. You're ready to let the cat choose the perfect order, but the cat is asleep, as usual, nesting in your shrinking pile of "keepers."

This section highlights some ways to rekindle your passions and your justifiable hopes. Get ready to dust off those pages, wake the cat, brew some fresh coffee, and do some things that will make a difference.

First of all, from reading manuscripts, teaching in more than two hundred poetry conferences, mentoring, talking with poets, and reading about 5,000 manuscripts each year, I know most poets focus almost endlessly on the idea of sequence. Countless poets think finding the perfect way to order the poems in a manuscript will make the crucial difference between acceptance and rejection, and the process of finding the right order means deciding exactly which poems to include or exclude.

Here's a wake-up call: Even in the "final" draft, poetry manuscripts are still works-in-progress, the individual poems are works-in-progress (yes, even if they've been published), and they will remain so right up to the time of the book's final proofing, and then again before your "New and Selected" volume comes out, and once more before your "Collected" edition hits Amazon's promised airborne delivery drones. (Skies filled with poetry; now there's a dream!)

As a publisher, I am concerned with the writing. I must love it. If the writing doesn't stun me with its freshness, with the genuine feel of risks taken, with discoveries made—if the writing doesn't make me want to—have to—keep turning the pages, then it matters very little what sequence you've chosen. Don't let poem order distract you from the more important task of making each poem a polished, exciting work unto itself. Concentrate all your renewed excitement, commitment, and effort at the level of the line (every line a poem). Then, at the level of the stanza. Then, at the level of the entire poem.

Where to go from here? Well, start by inviting yourself to explore your poems, one by one, as if a total stranger to them. Read them out loud, hear how your speaking voice responds to the inner voice of the poems. What discoveries do your poems suggest as you move through them? Trust that a poem is an exploration, even more so than you may already think you do. In what way might a sound suggest another sound, a word suggest another word, and that word imply a different sort of language, and that language signal a different way of thinking or feeling?

Certainly, finding the right mix of poems will lend a deeper resonance to all your poems, and that's a crucial, important step to take. You are an architect, building a book. Eventually. But you don't get to reward yourself with raising the roof beams until you have reentered the poems themselves. You're going to hate me for saying this, but it's a good idea at this stage of the process to simply assume that you don't actually yet have a book. If the book hasn't been taken by a publisher, though circulating forever, ten-to-one says it's not the order: it's the poems. Here, now, take time to imagine a place in which you can discover a deep, abiding, renewing patience.

Let me say it again: I'm suggesting that you start by rereading your work—each poem in your manuscript—out loud, to yourself, many times over, in your reading voice that's neither dramatic nor understated, that's as devoid of ego as it is interested in the sounds the lines make. I want you to be able to hear for yourself when you might be moving toward a discovery—something you didn't know when you started writing the poem, something you only dimly imagined being able to know.

Here are a couple of hints about how to determine key revisioning strategies for your own work. These are, admittedly, rather particularized responses to two rather generalized (if commonly shared) ways of writing.

Hint #1: If you tend to write lyrics that are heavily inflected with narrative elements, try forgetting what you know about making a story work. Forget scene setting. Forget character introductions. Forget telling the reader how you feel and how you see things. Rather, see if you can let those elements emerge from the way you describe gestures and summon metaphorical language.

In other words, try thinking of your poems as potent "dreamscapes" in which you, the speaker, "escape" into a place where some of the story is hinted at or sketched, but things do not necessarily need to add up, to make perfect sense—emotional or factual. See what happens when you permit yourself to revise your poems in a way that allows the dreamscape to take priority over the "story" you first imagined yourself telling. You can work toward this possibility by identifying and privileging evidence of all the senses your poem suggests to you. Paint, don't write, and your oils are images, your oils are the five senses, your oils are "risk" and "discovery," and your very own unconscious self.

Hint #2: If you tend to write either experimental or highly elliptical work, think about the place of pronouns in your poems. How the poem might use "gesture" to invite the reader in, and how it might use "gesture" to give the reader, even in a tenuous way, the shared experience of "having a look around the place." How might the poem make "place" itself signify in surprising ways, and then take leave of the reader in a way that leaves the reader transfixed, then altered. In other words, how will you create some element of dramatic tension where the element of "story" is subsumed? How will you take the chill out of the air? To what solid stuff will you tether your meditations, your language, your images, your questions?

In any case, see if you can locate what resonates with you and for you. Where is the poem warm, where is it cool? And as you do this hard, rewarding work, be ruthless with your choices. Just as you've bravely assumed that you may not actually have a manuscript yet (no matter how many pages are strewn around the room), you'll now even more bravely find the five or ten poems that resonate, that make even you say "wow." As you work on other poems, you may find that some earn their way into the book. You may find that in order to create a distinguished (and distinguishable) book, you'll want to be writing new poems. After all, if you do the hard work, you'll make discoveries, and those discoveries will lead to further exploration, and further exploration will lead to new poems, and those poems will cohere into a book that stands an exponentially improved likelihood of finding a home.

The Essential Work of Choosing the Right Poems

In point 3 of the section "The Art of the Manuscript," I made this statement: "Nothing could be less relevant to creating a manuscript than whether and where the individual poems found a home. If you believe in your poems, and if you have good reason for believing that they belong together in a particular manuscript, then include them, and order them according to your own aesthetic judgment. Period. If your poem published in the *New Yorker* doesn't work in this particular manuscript, save it for another book."

Can we talk for a few minutes about those last sentences?

I find that many poets I encounter in seminars, conferences, and on paper are eager to make journal editors who have taken this or that poem the arbiter of whether that poem is deserving. They apply hierarchical algorithms to the world of literary journals and magazines (this journal has a difficulty/esteem ratio of 3.5, that one a 7.2), to judge exactly how many points a published poem has earned—how many feathers for the cap.

Let's be honest. Would we really leave that poem we published in the *New Yorker* a year ago out of the manuscript we've charged, lightly armored, to defend the gates of Troy? Don't we want that weapon? That kudo? That cred?

We love the *New Yorker*. We worship the *New Yorker*. But, do we honestly agree with the aesthetic judgments of the *New Yorker*?

Of course we don't. How many times have we heard ourselves mutter, "Are they kidding with those poems? My two-year-old could write a better poem!" (Don't hold this against me, *New Yorker*. It's just, you know, humor. I love the *New Yorker*. I love everything about the *New Yorker*! Soon I will send you poems and I will pray to the gods that you take one, and my mother will paste it up on her refrigerator alongside Mary Oliver, and I will thenceforth only malign the aesthetic judgment of some less consequential litmag. Promise.)

But wait; let's indulge ourselves for a moment: Rejection sucks.

We hear the grief-laden stories and we ourselves contribute all the time—daily, really—to that Vast Edda of Rejection, which is the Void, which is the Destroyer of the Ego, which is the Legend of Incomprehensible Editorial Choices, which is the Reason for Flourless Chocolate Cake.

Social media is always buzzing with the lore of rejections and exhortations to perseverance, and of the merits of submission services and the advisability of multiple simultaneous submissions plotted against life-expectancy graphs, these tales leavened with the very occasional inspirational notes of triumph and consequential great relief and righteous celebratory just desserts of having one of our outliers taken on the forty-eighth try. As if.

As if all of our poems deserve, equally, to see the light of print, and in *Ploughshares* or the *Paris Review* at that. As if this particular lamb rejected as unworthy two dozen times now is, in fact, the potential Giver of Fire to Humankind.

Not so fast, sailor. By what right do we get to overlook our own narcissism and grandiosity? Do we really feel that getting a poem published on the forty-eighth try (or, for that matter, on the very first try) stamps said poem with the mark of deserved greatness? Is every poem we write a Worthy and Publishable Poem, ready to spring full-blown from the head of Zeus (or Hera)? Is every poem we fail to publish just another Sinner in the Hands of an Angry God? (Jonathan Edwards, really, no kidding.)

Maybe it was justly ignored. Maybe it was outrageously and unjustifiably ignored. Maybe we were lucky to get it published. Maybe we were lucky not to.

But enough. Are we adults here? Maybe we should go back to thinking about the book we're trying to make. Let's concentrate on which poems go into the book, and why.

Here's an idea. Take it for what it's worth. I don't know any two poets who conceive of a poem in the same way. Every time we write a poem, we announce to the world what a poem is. Poetry inhabits an enormous house, infinitely expanding to accommodate each of our unique sets of concerns—and we keep raising the roof and busting out the kitchen walls to make room for the ways in which we go about expressing and exploring what matters to us as writers.

The individual poems? We send them out into the world, the ones we love, and we hope that somebody loves them, too. The poem says, "Go ahead, make my day." And how we try to do justice to its imperative!

Therefore, build your audience by publishing all the poems you can. By all means, do that work. Communicating your poems with the world of readers is the essential underpinning of the art.

But the manuscript? That's a book you're making, and that book is a story that needs, first and mainly, to talk to you, and it talks to you only in the voices of its poems.

Practical Advice Coming: If you were to publish a book with Tupelo Press, we would send you an Author's Questionnaire, and among many other invasive questions, we would ask you to describe your book in a single sentence. And in a paragraph. And in a page. We would want to know that you know and can articulate what you write about, and how you write about it, and from what vantage point, and using what strategies.

We encourage our authors to express what matters to them in their poems. We want to know that they know what the matter is that comprises their poems. And why does what matters to them, matter to them? What makes the forty-six poems in their book work all of a piece? And how effectively do their choices of poetry-making strategies rub up against, buff and make shine, the concerns of their poems?

The Advice: I urge you to consider that it is beyond merely useful practice to try to answer these questions for yourself when you're putting the book of poems together. This is essential work. This is how you know what poems belong together. Really, this is the only way you'll know.

Putting the Book Together: A Little Bag of Suggestions

Ilya Kaminsky

Poem Number Twenty-Eight

"If the book contains twenty-seven poems," Robert Frost advised, "the book itself should be the poem number twenty-eight." I have heard this quote many times, but when I looked for it in Frost's letters and essays, I didn't find it. But the advice remains with me.

Why such a desire, such need, for the book of lyric poems to be anything more than the sum of its parts? Isn't a poem—if it's a good one—enough?

One good poem is certainly more than enough. And, yet, a reader, like any lover, cannot account for why they are obsessed with something, why they can't stop thinking about it, why they are in constant search for a book of poems that casts a spell, that requires one to sit down and to turn page, after page, after page.

So let me make this confession from the start: As a reader, I am one of those people obsessed with finding a book of poems that will make me want to read from the first page to last, without any possibility of stopping until it's done. I want to surrender myself completely to such a book, to such a voice.

But as a writer, one has to ask: How are such books able to keep their momentum over dozens of pages? What sequencing tools do their authors use? What can we, as fellow craftspeople, learn from them to construct a book of our own poems so that the book's structure or narrative or momentum will strengthen each individual poem?

Tools in Your Employment

I once had a chance to interview the brilliant short story writer, Grace Paley. *Grace,* I asked, *in your stories you have a reappearing character named Faith. Why does she appear in more than one story? What are you after with this?*

Her response: "Ah, Faith! Yes, Faith! Faith! I remember her. She works for me. She is in my employment."

The moral of the story: Everything you do in your writing, every decision you make, every poetic device you use is *in your employment.* Consider what kind of job they are performing. Can they do better on the level of your book?

For instance, what function are your titles performing in your book? Are they there just to label the poem? Are they contributing something new or unexpected to the poem? Or, perhaps, are they even helping to bring completely unrelated poems together?

Let's take a look at some of Jorie Graham's titles: "Self-Portrait as Apollo and Daphne," "Self-Portrait as Gesture Between Them," etc. What you notice first is the repeating, predictable "Self-Portrait" in each title. This gives you a sense of expectation; you turn the page in part because of the pattern's momentum. Of course, the second part of the title surprises you: The lyric moment of "Gesture Between Them" gives you something unpredictable, even mysterious. That's the payoff you get from turning that page. And now, you're hooked.

Another example of this style of titling comes from Anne Carson's book *Short Talks* (Brick Books, 1992), specifically from her sequence, "Life of Towns," where you can find "Apostle Town," "Town of Spring Once Again," "Lear Town," etc. Carson is the kind of poet who likes to bring unexpected things together, to see if there are any sparks when such things clash. Which is to say: She brings together a toy truck, a needle, a nuclear explosive, and a sidewalk. For the sequence to still feel cohesive, she needs structures that allow those opposites to coexist in some sensible, but not overtly obvious, form. Sequencing via titles allows for that. "Towns are the illusion that things hang together somehow, my pear, your winter," Carson writes. "I am a scholar of towns, let God commend that." Reading this description, you might think: *Oh, but in twenty seconds I will be able to predict what comes next.* Not at all. The predictability of titles is countered by the freshness and strangeness of content. The reader is constantly put on edge.

Other poets use their titles as a way to unite the book about a particular persona. For example, Zbigniew Herbert's late 20th-century classic, *Mr. Cogito* (1974; English translation Ecco Press, 1995), uses titles to introduce us to the recurring persona of Mr. Cogito: "What Mr. Cogito Thinks about Hell," "Mr. Cogito Seeks Advice," and so on. These titles might seem predictable, but the poems go wild, taking you to places as different as politics, metaphysics, laugh-out-loud humor, and off-hand comments on the poet's life.

Moving from books that use titles as structural tools to books organized around characters, we could think of Geoffrey Hill's *Mercian Hymns* (Deutsch, 1971), focusing on the mythical figure of the ancient English king, or Victoria Chang's *Barbie Chang* (Copper Canyon, 2017), a book that centers the life of the 21st-century Asian American mother. Or consider Rita Dove's haunting book-length lyrical narrative *Tomas and Beulah* (Carnegie Mellon University Press, 1986), which tells the story of her African American family in a racist country. Surprisingly, Dove's book contains few narrative poems. Instead, she's able to arrange the lyrics around the two characters so well, in such surprising ways, that the collection becomes a recognizable narrative. Or, you could build your book around a community instead of an individual, giving you the chance to sound various voices and perspectives, such as Dylan Thomas's *Under Milk Wood*.

If you write formal poems, you might consider: What's the function of form in your work? What are the villanelles, ghazals, sestinas, etc., doing for your larger project? In his very narrative (and wonderful) book *The Sugar Mile* (Houghton Mifflin Harcourt, 2005), Glyn Maxwell places a bunch of sestinas throughout the book. Why? The book is about New York City around 9/11 and London around the Blitz. It is punctuated by main characters going to a bar, where a lot of stories are told. And all the bar scenes are sestinas, serving the function of identifying a specific place, wherein the content can surprise us by its different tonalities within the form. This is an example of a poet taking full advantage of his formal capacities. He doesn't work for the form. The form works for him.

Against Narrative

"I don't want to tell stories," the great Brazilian poet Adelia Prado tells us, "stories are the excrement of time." Fair enough. If you're not interested in narrative order or the patterned expectation we've discussed, how can you bring a lyric structure to your book?

Wanda Coleman's lovely image comes to mind as one possible answer: "The order in which I prefer to place my poems often resembles a wave. The poem-action rises and falls, ebbs and flows." Then there is the age-old format of a book of hours—a collection of lyric poems, organized as a book of prayers, like Rilke's *Book of Hours*, or Louise Glück's *Wild Iris* (HarperCollins, 1992). Lucille Clifton also uses this form, with fascinating results.

Or you could consider organizing your book as a kind of stained-glass window, wherein the collection forms a frame for each individual, brilliantly colored bit of lyric glass. This might entail echoing connections between poems through repeated language, image, or structure that puts poems in dialogue with one another without using narrative. A good example of that is Li Young Lee's *Rose* (BOA Editions, 1993), an elegiac collection of poems about Lee's father. The book has an invocation and a final poem, which are in conversation with each other. The first and third sections are made up of short poems. The last poem of the first section is called "Eating Together," echoed by the first poem of the third section, "Eating Alone." Meanwhile, the second section, which is the center of the book, is a long rhapsodic poem called "Rose." So, the title of the book is drawn from this long piece in the middle, while the first and last section echo each other.

The form of the abecedarian is another way of organizing a book without narrative. Putting your poems into alphabetical order by first word or some other marker might lead to many unexpected discoveries. Poets who have used abecedarian across collections include Harryette Mullen, in *Sleeping with the Dictionary* (University of California Press, 2002), and Mary Jo Bang, in *The Bride of E* (Graywolf, 2009). Carolyn Forché's fourth book, *Blue Hour* (Harper, 2003), includes a very long incantatory abecedarian poem, "On Earth," another wonderful example. "On Earth" deals with the poet's childhood and her many travels abroad into conflict zones: It is a poem of many journeys, yet the one that is most important is that which you discover as the poem proceeds, through the English alphabet, following its own trials and revelations.

It is also worth noting that a book can collapse under the weight of an overly elaborate structure. There are several dangers; the pattern might be so repetitive that the reader becomes bored, or so intricate that the reader loses the threads that weave it together. But too often, this comes from a lack of clarity of vision in the structure, not from the fact of the structure itself.

Silence and Space

Consider silence. Consider section breaks. Consider the design of poems on the page.

Elizabeth Bishop's last book, *Geography III* (Farrar, Straus and Giroux, 1976), is designed to expand twenty-five to thirty pages of actual text into a book-sized manuscript. How? Examine the placement of her poems on the page. Consider how space is used between poems. Look at University of Chicago's Phoenix Poets series from the late 1980s and early 1990s. Notice how in these books there is quite a bit of space between the poem and the title. This space helps most page-long poems become two-page-long poems. But more importantly, it creates a bit of silence around the poems. The words have more space to sink in, so to speak.

Envoi: On Brevity

How many poems by your favorite poet do you consider life altering? Twenty? Thirty? Aspire to make a book of poems wherein each poem is someone's life-altering piece. Give us only your best. And not a page longer.

Don't add dozens of poems just to fit your structure. Even if I don't like its structure, I will buy a book of poems if I like at least five poems in it. Five really good poems—and I buy the book. That's my rule.

Finally: Don't push yourself for the sake of pushing. Go with the love of language, with music, go with what excites your senses. Start with poems that do those things, grow from your best work, and only add what can actually live up to your best work. I am reminded of Maggie Anderson's advice, let it have the last word:

"I know I am on my way toward a new book of poems when I have accumulated thirteen poems in a stack. . . . These are my rituals, my superstitions. When poets talk about assembling a book of poems, we like to suggest that it is an occult procedure. . . . *I write for myself and strangers,* as Gertrude Stein famously said. Dressing up a book of poems for public consumption may seem to smack of crowd-pleasing, sycophancy, or insufficient attention to the pure call of the inner voice. But the unconscious too, as we know, has its rigid orders."

The Art of Stumbling Upon

Cassandra Cleghorn

I found myself in the midst of completing a new poetry manuscript, but it felt like my first experience of truly making, rather than assembling, a book. I've heard many people say that their first book was a compilation, a more or less coherent grouping of the best poems they had written. What holds the first book together is often the set created by newly tested techniques, objects of attention, and stories that press themselves into service as one is learning one's craft.

There are exceptions, of course—Emma Hine's electric debut, *Stay Safe* (Sarabande, 2020) stands out as a recent example—but the model of the first book as catch-all matches my own experience of writing *Four Weathercocks*. The manuscript evolved over several years as my sheaf of poems grew and changed, but ultimately, the book's profile *as* a book derived quite directly from its thirty-four wide-ranging poems.

I'd like to switch the focus from "getting the book out" to something more like "stumbling upon the book." I invite you to suspend the concern about making a publishable collection, and the practical questions that follow: how to organize and order its contents, how to create the right titles and subtitles, how to identify suitable publishers, how to pitch the book, etc. I ask you to put on hold the ideas you have become attached to—about nailing down the main subject or theme or problem or project of your book.

Instead, I invite you to consider manuscript making as a profound opportunity to hone the art of stumbling upon. As I see it, *our task in making a book is to open ourselves to the possibility that the book we set out to write is somewhere to the side of the book we will end up making*. What follows are a few suggestions about how to encourage such openness in oneself. Rather than "mining" our work for its gleaming potential, or "wrestling" a manuscript into submission, might we instead open ourselves to the mysteries of process? What is cast off when we embrace unknowing? What happens when we allow ourselves to stumble upon what we haven't yet imagined?

In this alternate model, you yourself are the primary audience, and perhaps a small number of your most intimate readers: those whom you can trust to join you in the creative mining that results from proposing questions you can't yet answer. In this model, manuscript making provokes *inquiry, introspection, and improvisation*. How do the poems that already exist evoke as-yet-undiscovered revisioning, and even unwritten poems? And how do these new rewrites and new poems bump up against their forerunners to bestir an as-yet-nonexistent book?

I'm not thinking here about "project books." Kathy Fagan's latest book, *Sycamore* (Milkweed, 2017), for example, grew out of her obsession with the trees in her neighborhood. She told an interviewer that she was "so drawn to them that [she] geeked out on sycamore tree facts, doing research, following the appearance of sycamore in myth, legend, and the arts" (https://www.thecloudyhouse.com/2017/03/02/kathy-fagan-sycamore/). "I became interested in recording the trees in conversation with the weather, the light, and the landscape," she said, "with both natural and human history." In the midst of Fagan's single-minded focus, a long-term relationship came to an abrupt end. "I turned to the trees—and to the poems—for shelter," she said. "And both accommodated me." Fagan was blessed by her fascination. Her *idee fixe* of the sycamore tree proved endlessly congenial to a rich set of subjects, which "rose out of an underworld of sadness." Consistently orienting herself to the sycamore's (ostensibly) nonhuman life form, Fagan produced a collection of wildly inventive poems that seem all of a piece. (You can read more about her compositional strategies in the essay that follows.)

But most poets work from a less clearly delineated focus. My muse in this regard is Joanne Kyger (1934–2017), a much-underappreciated poet, who was close friends with Jack Spicer, Robert Duncan, Gary Snyder, Michael McClure, and Allen Ginsburg, but who also eschewed affiliation with the schools and movements these poets represented.

Kyger's books are marvels of spontaneity, even as they reflect her highly evolved craft. On the often-spare pages of her journal, Kyger refined the practice of "the editing that goes on in the ear." A mere five lines may suffice for the day's work, but those lines must bear witness to the moment—and motive—of their making. "If you can't read your own writing back," she told an interviewer, "it's time to find out what or how you want to write things."

I keep Kyger's books close to hand, inspired by her discipline and patience, by her readiness to train her sharp ear on herself, and by the trust she places in her instincts. Following her example, I shuffle poems, listening for the subvocal pings and unexpected resonances that might emerge from new juxtapositions. At the intersections and in the overlaps, new poems may suggest themselves. This kind of listening encourages improvisation and play. Kyger earned the nickname "Miss Kids" from her characteristic way of entering a room—"Hey, kids! I've got a great idea!" Kyger's lightness of touch reminds me to relax my tendency to bear down on the fledgling poem.

Perhaps most important, in respect to making a manuscript, Kyger helps me resist the market mentality that can warp the writing of a poem—the felt need to hothouse an idea, rushing it to completion in the dream of publication. Kyger rejected "the ruthless and useless activity" of academia, and was dumbfounded by the very fact of the AWP (Association of Writers & Writing Programs). She was always attuned to the pragmatic—where one's food comes from and how to pay the rent—so as to enable the writing life. Like many of our contemporaries, Kyger was alarmed by "the crowded 'I'" and its "watch-my-mind gymnastics"—what poet Dana Levin calls "the ambition and yearning and doubting and shame." To those of us who share Kyger's sense of vulnerability, and to herself, Kyger offers the reassurance that "poetry's an ally itself": "A more open mind can bring out a little more space, a little more wonder, more congratulations, which is something I would like to do." (All of the above quotes can be found in Wave Books' 2017 compendium of Kyger's ephemera, *There You Are*, edited by Cedar Sigo, a great introduction to the poet.)

The idea of listening around one's poems brings to mind another creative model: Paulina Olivera (1923–2016), the musician and composer who developed the idea of "deep listening." (You can learn about her work from her detailed website, https://paulineoliveros.us/, and from the Center for Deep Listening, which carries on her work at Rensselaer Polytechnic Institute, where she taught for many years). Oliveros defined deep listening as a way to widen radically the field of perception, "a practice that is intended to heighten and expand consciousness of sound in as many dimensions of awareness and attentional dynamics as humanly possible." Deep listening is a means of connecting intricately with one's physical surroundings, a defense against distraction and media saturation, a meditative practice, and a portal to the experience of collectivity. "Take a walk at night," she suggested in one of her *Sonic Exercises* (1974), "Walk so silently that the bottoms of your feet become ears."

In the spirit of Oliveros' advice, you might pad barefoot through your manuscript as it evolves and changes, developing new weather systems, new growths and riffs, new architectural spaces. Listen for overtones and dissonances. Remembering that *stanza* means "room," open yourself to the possibility of redecoration or even structural renovation. Above all, know that deep listening is an empathetic act. Attune yourself to the poems that exist, and to the spaces around them, the vectors that connect them, and the shadows and refractions that appear.

Which brings us to the presence of ghosts in the making of a manuscript. Ruth Ellen Kocher's last several books were driven by the poet's interest in process. Her extraordinary book, *domina/un-Blued* (2013) remains one of my favorite Tupelo Press titles. Kocher describes the travail of writing and rewriting this book. In some respects, she courted difficulty. At that time, she was inspired by the documentary *The Five Obstructions* (2003), in which filmmaker Lars von Trier tasked his mentor, Jorgen Leth, to remake his short film, *The Perfect Human*, five times, each revision under the constraint of a new "obstruction" devised by von Trier. In an interview with Oliver de la Paz, Kocher said,

"After watching it two or three times I realized that nothing about my approach to the page had ever brought me to the brink of tears. The idea that creative despair could yield something I might not otherwise imagine—it was seductive. That documentary inspired my process in *domina Un/blued*. For that project, I wanted to figure out how to use destruction as a form of obstruction."

Kocher's long-term revision process involved painstaking cutting and rearranging of the text, with often uncanny results. Poems would reform before her eyes, reverting in form, reshaping themselves in ways that felt beyond her control. "I'm attracted to projects with some structural free-for-all that feels a little impossible," says Kocher. In order to do the work of the impossible, she first loosens her hold. She stumbles to the brink, and then listens deeply for how to recover through invention.

These, then, are what I consider to be key parts of the process of stumbling upon a manuscript: slowing down, staying open, shuffling, listening deeply, reinventing—to let go of the bearing down, but to go limp, opening yourself to . . . .

World-Building Your Poetry Manuscript

Kathy Fagan

A short stack of useful advice gets served to poets putting together their first books. I've offered the same practical suggestions to MFA students and others: front load your manuscript with the most affecting poems that introduce your manuscript's primary concerns, organize the work in order to achieve point(s) and counterpoint(s), begin each section with a strong poem that deepens the work appearing before it, close the manuscript with poems that illuminate and, if possible, extend the manuscript's thematic and formal explorations.

I know poets who love putting manuscripts together, poets who are truly great editors of their own and others' work, but I am not one of those poets. What draws me to a manuscript that I might choose for a publication prize is the very same thing that commands my attention in published books, in MFA theses, and in my own inexpert attempts to organize my manuscripts: evidence of world building and the invitation—some sense of welcome, some yielding to the pressures of an audience, real or imagined—to enter that book's world.

For me, world building begins with the process of generating material—notes, research, experimentation, an openness to various obsessive paths. Over the course of my lifetime, this process has grown into an evolving aesthetic, or set of aesthetics, that is specific to the creation of my own, very different, six books. What follows is an analysis of those methods, in the hope that something here speaks directly to your experience of building a world in your poetry manuscript.

On February 9, 1914, Gypsy Rose Lee, the famous burlesque performer, was born. On February 9, 1957, my parents were married. Ecdysiast is another word for stripper. My parents divorced in the mid-'80s, I can never remember the year. My dementing, destitute father moved in with me in 2014; my mother died in 2017. The kind of story-puzzle or emotional complex that these facts build together echoes the structural puzzle—and the elements of drama (convergence and coincidence), pathos, and joke rhetoric—I'm drawn to as a poet. In other words, how a world gets built from these elements.

It's been said of the composer John Cage that he "devises ingenious systems to build structures from dumb abundance." A stage is one of our most basic structures. It's defined most simply as a raised platform. Goethe said, "stage means the universe." Montaigne, "the whole vast universe serves for a theater." Shakespeare wrote, of all living things, "they have their exits and their entrances."

Stage also suggests travel, a journey, a level or degree (as in stagecoach, flood stage, or stage 2 malignancy). The level at which material is observed under a microscope is called a stage. There are stages in the fields of aerospace, geology, electronics, architecture, and engineering. I don't think about all this when I'm making a poem or book, but I do think about Linda Gregerson's essay in which she says that the rhetorical contract the lyric poet makes with a reader relies on their existing in the fiction of the poem a one-time speaker engaging a one-time audience ("Rhetorical Contract in the Lyric Poem," *Kenyon Review*, Spring 2006). In other words, Gypsy Rose Lee may have been a stripper, but what her audience witnessed was not *that* woman naked; she didn't do self-revelation so much as the revelation of *a* self, the performance of a persona.

When I began writing poems seriously, I wanted to tell, or sing, my family's stories: immigrant stories, neighborhood stories, childhood stories, my own love songs and laments. The nostalgia and declarations of my first book, *The Raft* (Plume, 1985), are appropriate only to one as young as I was when the poems were composed. I wouldn't say my later poems are anticonfessional. In fact, once I quit imposing myself *on* or composing myself *in*to my poems, they may have become more rather than less autobiographical. However, I will say that the work after my first book became as interested in looking outward as inward, interested in others, in character, in the environment, in history and language. I still wanted to sing, but no longer strictly a "song of myself," to borrow a phrase.

Philip Larkin says in an essay that the poem is a "verbal device that will reproduce an emotional concept in anyone who cares to read it." Because I was so enmeshed over the long period of time it took to write my second book, *MOVING & ST RAGE* (University of North Texas Press, 1999), in elegy and the various raw emotions that motivate the elegiac mode—my best friend died tragically young, to which I responded with a long uncomfortable silence—I had to explore structure and voice more deeply. Left to the methods of poem making and thinking that were familiar to me, my work became mired in the facile and self-indulgent. I needed the "slant" perspective Dickinson speaks of; the good strangeness that can only be achieved through, as I envision it, a turning outward via paths of metaphor, image, voice, conscious form, and persona. Research into medieval iconography provided me with a loose framework to work within, and writing experiments, the weirder the better, offered me the serious play I needed to focus my interest.

For me, there's always existed a direct parallel between the elegiac mode and the impulse to create verse opportunities for speakers or characters other than myself. *Sycamore* (Milkweed, 2017), for instance, my fifth book, uses the figure of the tree as a focus for my grief after the abrupt and brutal end of my sixteen-year relationship. In the title poem of my second collection, something lost—the letter "O" in the word storage—becomes the reason for the archetypal lovers, Moving and St Rage, to come into existence at all. The notion of the missing letter led me to the medieval practice of illumination, the ornate decoration of alphabetical letters in books of prayer, such as the famous Book of Kells. Having grown up Catholic, I was compelled to continue that research, discovering the iconographic meanings of other familiar symbols from my youth: carnations, finches, unicorns, all the flora and fauna that held, for believers who could not read, a story that I, centuries later without a key, could only intuit.

It is perhaps no coincidence that as I labored over the final stages of this difficult book, both elegiac and myth heavy, I fell in love and came out. The language of both new romance and profound loss is a coded one, borne of an elaborately structured, deeply private, solitary sort of magical thinking. Imaginary friends are one result of this thinking, as is religious fervor and extremism of most kinds. I've learned that these conditions, usually temporary, engender art because like the artist they are obsessive, providing artists with stores of material, entire cosmologies. An unnamed Ozark woman in the final section of this book—my friend was from the Ozark region of Missouri, though she is not *this* woman—literally interrupts a long personal elegy to rant at me, the book's author, and tell her own stories. Formally and thematically, I was interested, I saw as the manuscript finally came to completion, in charm and trickery. Like Houdini or the teller of *Arabian Nights*, I understood that the purpose of performance, love, and art is to defy death.

Sycamore has an emotional connection to *MOVING & ST RAGE*, which ultimately took fourteen years to finish. The loss behind *Sycamore* was equally gutting for me, but it generated poems rather than shutting them down. If silence was the reply I'd made to my friend's death, poetry was the reply I made to what I felt would be my own.

I've thought a lot about these two responses to loss—my age had something to do with each of them—but I remember feeling slammed closed when my friend died and broken open when my marriage did. What I mean is, there was light and air for me in the second loss. It didn't matter that it was winter light, and the air was so cold it hurt my lungs; I wrote in the kind of fever that writers envy and fear. I lived for my poetry and my trees. When the fever broke, I had a book to make, and that was about discovering how the sycamore poems and the speaker's grief were related—they are, more subtly in the book than in my life, but it took me a little time and therapy to figure out how.

My third book, *The Charm* (Lynx House, 2012), was in every way an antidote to the grief explored in the previous book. Written and published quickly, it investigates the magic and terrors of childhood, casting little spells or charms to ward off fear, loss, and death. I wanted to avoid the formulaic expression of "the spell" as the poems were being made, focusing instead on a range of poem utterances and modes. Part of "the charm" for me of this manuscript was finding a way to keep the tone or the voice of the poems relatively consistent while experimenting more widely than ever before with humor, form, and register. I wanted to be true to the child's experience of both terror and pleasure during play (or reading, learning, growing up), and to that end I felt I needed to "discover" my way through the poems in a sort of freefall. It was a short-lived book—the press folded only months after *The Charm*'s publication—but I remain grateful for the joy it gave me and a few readers, and for the opportunity to invite new processes of composition into my life.

In fact, it was research for a small poem on Joseph Cornell appearing in that collection that provided me the bridge between books three and four, though I didn't know it at the time. Cornell was a renowned hermit and maker of surrealist assemblages who lived with his mother all his life in Queens, where I was born. Most of his boxes were dedicated to famous women: Emily Dickinson, Marianne Moore, Lauren Bacall, and others. Found in his papers after his death were what he called "dossiers," or portfolios full of notes on and images of various women, many of them ballerinas. I'd already been researching women's cosmetics of the nineteenth and twentieth centuries, much of which was originally created by and for women on the stage, most of whom were considered far less respectable than the stripper, Gypsy Rose Lee. At the same time (by coincidence?), I was attending many opera and dance performances. I also routinely indulge an abiding interest in the dramatic lives of the saints, Joan of Arc in particular, and several biblical figures, mainly women. The convergence of these interests very easily suggests the metaphor of the performer onstage.

However, eventually I realized, over the course of several books, that it was no longer stage (structure) and persona (voice) that held my attention exclusively; it was what I began to think of as understructure and undervoice—and how these two elements lead to the surprising inevitable in poems. Literally, how what goes on backstage or beneath the structure, and what is held just under the voice or withheld by persona, will reveal, by way of clockworks, ropes, and pulleys, the acrobatic mysteries of the psyche.

I subscribe to T. S. Eliot's notion that genuine poetry communicates before it is understood (that it is apprehended before it is comprehended). But how to do that when the poetry you're writing is about what's expertly hidden and rarely if ever communicated? Which I believe is the condition of most poetry. Cornell did it in his art through what he called "metaphysique d'ephemera," the metaphysics of the ephemeral. He built boxes from scrap wood and filled them with five-and-dime toys and collage images cut out of celebrity magazines—your basic junk. The result is campy and haunting. "Dossier," a word all too familiar to academics, comes from the homely old word "dorser" from the sixteenth century, a kind of purse or improvised package of valuables, usually covertly sewn into hems or rags. One kind of dorser is the stick with the bundle tied to the end of it carried over one's shoulder, your classic tramp bag. It's the most rudimentary luggage or, to put it in colloquial terms, the baggage we carry with us every day into every exchange. We've all got baggage: pain, insight, wisdom, issues, experience—whatever you wish to call it; turning it into art is what separates artists from other humans.

My fourth collection, *Lip* (Carnegie Mellon University Press, 2009), at first appears to swing entirely away from personal matters; it's a collection of persona poems. I did extensive research for *Lip*, and built different kinds of poem vessels in it. It felt imperative in the years I spent making those poems to immerse myself in thoughts other than my own. My aim, not fully articulated to myself until later, was to disobey the workshop command, "Write about what you know." I simply needed to know more. And the only way to achieve that for one like me was to read—history books, dance books, art books—letting the burrs of knowledge, to paraphrase Frost, stick to my socks as I walked through the fields willy-nilly. The rebellion against authority, queerness, working-class upbringing, and outlier status I had tried so hard for so long to outgrow stoked the fire in which these poems were forged. The book, however, required me to speak the poems largely through others: transgressive historical figures, mostly subversive women, real and imagined. I still do a great deal of research for my poems, but the truest work is largely internal now.

Poet and activist Audre Lorde says in her life-altering book, *Sister Outsider* (Crossing Press, 1984), that poets turn their pain into art. Her willingness in her poems and essays to discuss poetry and raw emotion changed me forever as a poet. Or, rather, they returned to me the moment when I had discovered poetry and why it held for me then and continues to hold for me now, that mixture of mystery and truth, with the power to sustain me through any life crisis.

When I was making my book *Sycamore*, for example, I realized that I didn't want it to be "just about" trees any more than I wanted it to be "just about" a bad break-up. I wanted the poems to tell a larger story together, but not a story that moved in any linear way, which feels false to my experience. What that left me was a much more naturally cyclical, seasonal way to organize the material. I was conscious of beginning the book in winter, when my relationship ended—and, in keeping with the mythic undertones of that, balancing midwinter with midsummer, the invisible with the visible, and the young with the old. I hoped that the two overarching events of the book (the speaker's grief and tree studies) would weave in and out of the whole, allowing for discovery alongside recovery. One of the reasons I adore the image that my publisher, Milkweed, gave to the cover of *Sycamore* is its aerial perspective. The photograph is taken from above, and the objects photographed evoke tree tops—or barbed wire, or brain synapses. The poems spend so much time on the ground (or, in many cases, under the ground), that there had to be a vertical movement upward, too, a literal branching. The three sections of the book provided the space or air, it seems to me, to promote multiple perspectives.

The sycamores felt to me emotionally sheltering during a very difficult time. They still do, like the best imaginable (giant) family, but the poems themselves mostly rose out of the darkest places, an underworld of sadness—my own "comas of survival," as I put it in the poem "To You for Whom I Broke." Poetry and psychotherapy plumb multiple layers of understanding. Likewise, one can't stand at the base of an old-growth sycamore looking up and not feel both terribly mortal and entirely bound up in history all at once. The ultimate in negative capability, hibernation is the life-death state, one in which survival and death are completely interdependent—Daphne, Persephone . . . . The resonances are endless.

Aside from Ovid's *Metamorphosis,* the poems in *Sycamore* draw from arts other than the literary, like film (Fellini and Herzog are credited in the book) and video (the Gaillard demolition video that the poem "Cinder" engages), dance (ballet and Kabuki), sculpture (Bernini, of course), architecture (the destroyed and the extant; there's a poem about California's first woman architect, Julia Morgan), and even music, which to my uneducated ear reads as almost pure abstraction and emotion. Experiencing all the arts is so often visceral for me that it becomes as influential as narrativized experience and certainly as influential as any craft I learned in poetry school. As usual for me, there's a mash-up of characters in the poems, too, aside from the individual and choral groups of trees: many, many saints, Caesar Augustus, Edgar Poe, Alice Toklas, Virginia Woolf, and Michael Jackson, to name a few. Travel has also allowed me to see sycamores and their cousins thrive along the Tiber in Rome, and the Seine in Paris, cities that I can't help but equate with the visual art found in them. I took hundreds of photos of the trees with Monet's studies in mind. I also like to think of poems as constructions, like Leonardo's inventions, each created as experiments devoted to different purposes. Finally, it's language(s) and weathers that these *Sycamore* poems have made themselves from; seasons of listening to and watching everything, including art.

Which brings me to this moment. Recently, I submitted my sixth manuscript, tentatively titled *Bad Hobby*, to my publisher, and the composition and arrangement of the poems are still fresh in my mind.

I am a slow, nonprolific writer, but adopting some strategies from creative nonfiction helped me to make poems while also holding down a demanding job and caretaking for my dementing dad in my home. The braided essay, for example, which allows for several threads of experience at once, complicating the primary narrative; the lyric possibilities in plainspoken facts; the willingness—connected to psychotherapy—to engage memory and trauma more directly than one might expect in a poem, relying on the art to be rendered instead by attention to detail, poem structures (including sentence and line), and meanings made via sound (cadence and rhythm). While these poems are absolutely autobiographical, as well as researched, I was amazed that the speaker of the poems was always most definitely an "I" aware of the occasion of the poem, and, as the manuscript progressed, aware of the overall presentation of the world I was making in the poems. That world was not the one in which I fed and clothed my dad every day and taught my classes, but the world in which I processed the present with memory, my own childhood with intergenerational trauma, my specific parents and grandparents with their historical and political moments, and my labor with the labor of women across borders and time.

It was my therapist, for instance, who recommended that for my new manuscript I read Herodotus's *The Histories*, specifically passages on the habitual sale of women and the excruciating hierarchies of such purchases. I'd already found Aristotle's writing on animal prudence, the title of one poem in the new manuscript, which inspired further research into predation. From there to monthly visits with my father to the VA clinic, to research in falconry, and my obsessive tracking of AccuWeather reports (its "Real Feel" temperatures and Daily Hunting Forecasts, for example), I've learned many little lessons in language, gender, health, reproduction, and survival as commodity, painfully relevant to all of us.

Organizing the poems was challenging in a different way. I had more material than I typically do when I organize a manuscript. I had to read *for* the book to decide what stayed and what had to go. What forwarded and deepened my book's project—poet as the aging child of dead/dementing parents, herself childless—and what didn't. There were very short and very long poems in the manuscript that required different levels of attention. The grandparent poems, poems of childlessness, and poems that addressed directly and indirectly the predation that the structures of art and family perpetrate on their participants and the planet. It took two overall iterations to get me to contract, and I suspect there will be another iteration between contract and publication. The organizational concerns for me were twofold: contextualizing the family dynamic in non-prosaic ways and pacing the drama(s) of the book so that the triangulation of subject matters (the manuscript is in three sections for reasons specifically to do with content) held somewhat equal roles.

There were a handful of poems in the manuscript, for example, that had merit and needed, for the reasons above, to stay, but each time I read them I found myself disengage. I knew, reluctantly, that if I disengaged a reader would, so I repurposed that material altogether. One poem was subsumed by a longer poem, the longer poem was trimmed and reconfigured into a part-prose/part-verse poem, and another set of poems lost a few companions to become a suite of poems with greater cohesiveness. I think a willingness to think in terms of the whole, along with a certain nimbleness of mind—which again, I thank nonfiction and visual artists for—can enhance both project books and collections of poems much more satisfactorily than an inflexible devotion to a single principle of organization. Such willingness and nimbleness provide the complexity and textures that I, for one, find so appealing in the books I return to most often.

The Power of the Unsaid in Poetry: On Silence, Rupture, and Unexpected Shifts

Kristina Marie Darling

Silence as an Invitation to the Reader

In "The Metaphysics of Youth," Walter Benjamin observes that "[c]onversation strives toward silence, and the listener is really the silent partner. The speaker receives meaning from him; the silent one is the unappropriated source of meaning." In other words, it is the space between words that sets off language, the dim background against which a light becomes visible. For Benjamin, silence was the precondition for a community out of which story arises, and the vast expanse waiting just beyond its inevitable end.

Here I'll examine three collections of poetry that fully do justice to this complex relationship between silence, narrative, and the tacit relationships out of which language is born. Julie Marie Wade's *When I Was Straight* (A Midsummer Night's Press, 2014), Eileen G'Sell's *Life After Rugby* (Gold Wake Press Collective, 2018), and Rajiv Mohabir's *The Taxidermist's Cut* (Four Way Books, 2016) each consider, albeit from vastly different conceptual vantage points, the ways silence makes possible our experience of beauty, that "gift of dark lace" woven into each poem. For G'Sell, Mohabir, and Wade, the possibility of transcendence resides in the space between things, and it is always a bright aperture that gives rise to a "queer flutter that knocks about your ribs." Though vastly different in style and sensibility, these three books share an investment in allowing opulence to be complemented by the reader's own unspoken imaginative work and contemplation, offering us only "the sound of boots through snow and the dark."

What's more, these writers show us a full range of approaches to what silence can do. In G'Sell's dense, image-driven lyrics, this purposeful withholding often takes the form of absent narrative scaffolding. What is left unsaid becomes an invitation to the reader, a pathway into the book's rich fictive terrain. For Mohabir and Wade, however, each aperture manifests as a kind of rupture, a subtle violence done to voice and language. As Mohabir tells us, "Every time you speak they hear a different hell."

One Variation: Silence as a Purposeful Withholding of Context

In *Life After Rugby*, each line is dense in its presentation of images, types of rhetoric, and vibrant soundscapes. For G'Sell, this disconcerting proximity—of images, of lexicons, and of narratives—gives rise to countless elisions, as the relationships, the rules that govern this imaginative topography, are often left to the reader's imagination. Indeed, we are offered "a cheekbone shyly brushing your wrist," though the speakers of these poems rarely tell us to whom a body, or an encounter, belongs.

In many ways, silence is intricately linked to pacing in this work, as the speed with which we transition does not afford time or space for exposition. It is the breathlessness of each poem, their restless movements and their dense, complex music, that allows silence to inhabit them so fully. Indeed, the relationships, the associations, and the resonances are too numerous to count. Reminiscent of Joshua Clover's *The Totality for Kids* (University of California Press, 2006) and Kathleen Peirce's *The Ardors* (Ausable/Copper Canyon, 2004), G'Sell's poems also fearlessly confront, through their satisfyingly dense constructions and their quick, unpredictable leaps, our own discomfort with silence, while at the same time gesturing at its inevitability. G'Sell elaborates:

> With the best of her Sugar Ray Leonard bob,
> She weaved beyond traffic.
> Symphony, prosperity, the loose mares of time.

Homily of hominy, the long dreams and lime.
Outside her glowing loungecar, igloos in space.

In many ways, these lines might be read as an ars poetica, as G'Sell gestures at the work's own "symphony" of disparate images, lexicons, and miniature soundscapes. In passages like this one, the reader begins to see that the poems are constructed against silence, but also that the poems exist because of that negative space. The absence of narrative scaffolding and all that is left unsaid allow the story to grow wilder.

Another Variation: Silence as Politically Charged

Mohabir's poetry reads as a novel take on G'Sell's exploration of silence, elision, and readerly unease. While formally diverse, spanning tercets, couplets, and hybrid experiments, *The Taxidermist's Cut* is gracefully unified by an exploration of silence as a kind of violence, a rupture in the faultlessly woven tapestry of voice, narrative, and community. Mohabir writes, "Knowledge / of Violence: / where welts rose on my legs / from the riding crop hidden / by your headboard, / the crumble of song / shuddered in my hands." Here, lineation, and its ensuing pauses, exists in tension with the sentence as well as with the syntactic unit. Clauses (like "knowledge of violence" and "hidden by your headboard") are halved by Mohabir's deft and provocative lineation. When read through the lens of the book's exploration of cultural otherness, these stylistic gestures take on a new and conceptually arresting significance, as Mohabir shows us that silence—in poetry, in culture, and in our own consciousness—is politically charged.

Through his accomplished craft and thoughtful approach to style, Mohabir shows us the myriad ways that censorship and the fear, deeply rooted in our culture, of confronting difficult questions, is gradually internalized, shaping one's conscious experience even in solitude. This, Mohabir shows us, is the ultimate form of violence and intrusion. He elaborates:

Your parents are at Bible study, leaving you alone with the devil
    inside.
Your clothes are strewn about the floor.
The rain ricochets drops through the windowpane.
Your drops drone and soar from the opened window as cicadas.
Inside you rain. You are a forgery. Not a wolf. Not an Indian.
    Not a son.

What is particularly revealing in this passage is Mohabir's adept and skillful use of caesura. Here, the work's meaningfully timed pauses, the persistent stop and start, give rise to an uneasy, hesitant music (most visible in phrases like "as cicadas. Inside you rain."). We are shown that the voice of culture (which manifests powerfully in lines like "You are a forgery.") ultimately engenders silence, even in the speaker's uncontested solitude. Yet at the same time, Mohabir calls our attention to the music that silence allows us to hear. What's more, he reminds us of the persistence of voice, and of music, even as the voice of the establishment "drones" through "the opened window."

A Third Variation: Silence as a Dramatization of Injustice

Like Mohabir and G'Sell, Wade's poetry exists at the interstices of speech, silence, and unease. Presented as a book-length exploration of the speaker's life before she came out as a lesbian, the poems in this stunning collection are haunted by a kind of shadow story, a narrative that resides just beneath the surface of these lively, jocular poems. Like G'Sell's poetry, these pieces exist against silence and the confrontation—with selfhood, identity, and desire—that inevitably ensues.

As the book unfolds, each poem becomes a poignant dramatization of what's left unsaid. Yet at the same time, speech calls attention to its own artifice. Wade's poems are constantly gesturing, at turns playfully, knowingly, and sorrowfully, toward all that cannot, will not, be spoken aloud. "I could tell my mother how / I wanted her to brush my hair / &

braid it through with ribbons," Wade writes. "I could tell my father how / I loved baking cookies & / pinning damp clothes on the line." Here what is perhaps most revealing is the line break and ensuing pause before "pinning damp clothes on the line." The moments of elision, as in Mojabir's work, become politically charged, as Wade's speaker struggles to signify and perform an identity that is foreign to her. Through her silence, the speaker also experiences herself as foreign, and this, for Wade, is violence.

Yet she also shows us silence as agency, as manipulation of a cultural system and of readerly expectations. "I might have smiled more then," Wade writes, "the part of my lips so often mistaken / for happiness. In fact, it was something else— // a fissure, a break in the line—the way / a paragraph will sometimes falter / until you recognize its promise as // a poem." In much the same way that Wade's speaker masquerades in her interactions with others, the moments of rupture and elision within the poem ultimately toy with the reader's preconceived ideas about how a narrative should or ought to unfold. Here the pause, that subtle and playful rupture before "a poem," the subsequent delay before narrative resolution, exemplifies the ways that silence in Wade's work gives rise to suspense, surprise, and wonder.

Indeed, that speechlessness engendered by culture is appropriated and recontexualized in a way that empowers the speaker, rather than censoring her. Like Mohabir and G'Sell, Wade shows us that each moment of elision contains multitudes. It is in these liminal spaces—the glowing aperture, the tentative sigh, the pause for breath—that the rules of language no longer hold, and anything becomes possible.

An earlier version of this essay appeared in *Ploughshares.*

Repetition as Voyage and Transfiguration

Kristina Marie Darling

An Introduction

I was initially resistant to Ben Lerner's *Mean Free Path* (Copper Canyon, 2010). After all, he does warn the reader that there is in the book "[n]othing for you here but repetition." The unvaried line lengths of these poems, and the seemingly constrained vocabulary of imagery, could easily appear as mere remnants of a failure of the imagination. Yet we tend to forget that any transformation begins with reiteration, as the phrase we recall is said and unsaid, memorialized and unmade at the same time.

With that in mind, Lerner reminds his reader that there is no such thing as "sameness" when considering an encounter with the poetic image. As his speaker moves through time, and as he is changed by its articulation of history, he discovers each "star," each "identical city," with a different mind and heart. Lerner helps us see repetition as an undeniable difference, as the "applause" and the "sedimented roar" are revisited on an individual who has fundamentally metamorphosed. We are made to hear his "voice" as both old and new, in much the same way that we are shown oneself as another.

Two other recent collections, Kristy Bowen's *Salvage* (Black Lawrence, 2016) and Elizabeth J. Colen's *What Weaponry* (Black Lawrence, 2016) offer startling variations on this framing of repetition as subtle transformation. In Bowen's gorgeously cinematic presentation of the poetic image, each "house made of mothers," each "house destroyed," functions as a projection, a portrait of a self that remains in a constant state of flux. We are shown ongoingness and becoming frame by frame, the poems functioning as stills of a heroine on screen, who never ceases moving. Similarly, Colen's recurrent imagistic motifs make provocative ontological claims. She calls our attention to the ways that repetition is often a process of estrangement, as each iteration of the same image bears us further and further afield.

Taken together, these three books raise what is essentially a question of limitation and possibility: How much transfiguration can the same mind, and the same finite world, sustain?

One Variation: Repetition as an Accumulation

In *Mean Free Path*, Lerner builds a "dark aisle" just to see how much "plain language" can fit within it without the door coming "unhinged." Each poem's construction represents both minimalistic restraint and egregious excess, as significance accumulates around every "disaster" revisited, every familiar and perilous "edge."

This notion of repetition as precarious architecture, as accumulation, and as necessary destruction, is enacted on both small and large scales. On the level of the individual poem, we see many very different types of repetition holding vastly divergent lines together. Taking the first poem after the dedication as an example, one observes sound (such as the alliteration that binds "delays" to "sensations," "audible" to "absence" and "rain"), syntax (particularly the subject-verb-object construction that links clauses like "Waiting is the answer" and "Any subject will do"), and of course, recurrent imagistic motifs.

These subtle gestures within each poem serve to mitigate the wild associative leaps that occur, as there are often ontological and syntactic worlds between one line (for example, "The audible absence of rain") and the next (the wildly divergent "Take the place of objects"). Repetition offers a way of closing gaps, but also, a way of transforming them, allowing each vast expanse bridged by "description" to become a "system," a "standing wave," enlivened by movement and slow, careful metamorphosis.

As these varied and various types of repetition intersect and overlap on the level of the larger sequence, their interlocking structure becomes metaphor, ultimately traversing the distance that is so elegantly described in these poems: "I'm writing this one / With my eyes closed, listening to the absence of..." Indeed, the imagistic motifs, syntactic structures, and alliterative gestures that recur throughout the sequence, and that bind one line to the next, begin to simulate proximity, despite the syntactic and metaphoric chasms that separate each line, poem, and page.

In many ways, it is this tension between distance and proximity that allows Lerner's framework to hold so many of the same "little contrasts" without becoming claustrophobic for the reader, as we are made to see each motif, each syntactic structure, from different emotional and intellectual vantage points. As Lerner himself writes, "Nothing's changed except the key."

Repetition as Architecture in a Manuscript

The most moving poems in Lerner's book address the absent other directly: "If you would speak of love / Stutter, like rain . . . " This unflinching lyricism allows us to understand how desire motivates these elaborate accumulations, the careful architecture that takes shape over the course of the book.

For Lerner, the love lyric becomes voyage and transfiguration, a landscape slowly and irrevocably transformed, just as the speaker is changed—by time, history, and the relationship itself. He writes:

> You startled me. I thought you were sleeping
> In the traditional sense. I like looking
> At anything under glass, especially
> Glass. *You* called *me*. Like overheard
> Dreams . . .

Although the pronoun "you" is reiterated throughout these lines, we are presented with vastly different facets of the same love object: She is at turns secretive (as she "startles" the speaker), somnambulant

("I thought you were sleeping"), and finally disconnected, prompting both clarification and denial ("*You* called *me*"). Indeed, repetition subtly suggests that distance and proximity inhabit the same moments. With each reiteration of the word "glass," we find ourselves at a greater remove, one step further from the desired narrative. The layers of "glass" multiply, concealing a version of the scene possibly more real and true. Just as the speaker likes "looking / At anything under glass, especially / Glass," we see both characters refracted and distorted through repetition. Yet this distortion is revealed as the truest representation of the dynamic between them, the impossibility of empathy and connection, and the knowledge that one can never fully inhabit the mind or heart of another.

In many ways, the moments of indirectness within the collection allow us to see Lerner's more direct pieces in sharper relief. When the glass reappears, as rubble ("axes to grind into glass") and as threshold ("sliding doors," "a poem through a windshield"), the speaker meets them alone.

Another Variation: Repetition as Politically Charged

Elizabeth J. Colen's *What Weaponry* offers a provocative variation on Lerner's envisioning of repetition as distance and proximity. For Colen, repetition is a process of making strange, bearing us farther and farther away from the familiar with each room revisited, each reiteration of the image we once thought we knew.

Much like *Mean Free Path*, *What Weaponry* utilizes many different types of repetition: parallel syntax, sound motifs, and a vocabulary of imagery that imposes its own willful constraints. Here sound and syntax, however familiar they may become, only heighten the wonderful strangeness of Colen's imagery. She writes in "Low Clouds":

> When we see it from above we will know the sea is near, as is the grey, as is the end. When we see it from above the plane will be circling, destroying low clouds. When we see it from above

> we will be listening, we will be watching, we will go there as fast as we can.

The quoted poem, the first in the collection, reads almost as ars poetica, instructing the reader how to approach the "circling" and recursive prose within the book. Here "the sea," which appeared earlier in the poem as "wet sand between our toes," has been rendered entirely other, functioning as a harbinger of destruction. Indeed, what makes "the sea" and the "low clouds" so disconcerting is the vantage point from which they are seen as the poem draws to a close: We slowly realize that we are falling. As the poem's "concentric circles grow," each return and reiteration is also a step toward the poem's unmaking. Though the "crabs" and "dry kelp" comprise a consistent vocabulary of maritime imagery, the vantage point from which it is seen becomes less and less safe. In this respect, Colen's work proves comparable to Lerner's, as the same image is presented at varying degrees of remove. Repetition for both writers is a voyage, an orbit around a deceptively stable center of gravity.

Repetition as a Dramatization of a Collection of Subthemes

What Weaponry is perhaps most powerful when this repetition becomes a kind of violence. Given the familiarity of the images and syntactic structures we encounter, this framing of the book's "talking in circles" as aggression, as threat, is all the more unexpected. In this respect, repetition is not only a source of structural unity within the book, it is a form of resistance, a sly and subtle feminist practice.

Throughout *What Weaponry*, we are presented with "mornings [that] stab the breath right out of our lungs." Yet the speaker of these poems is also implicated in this destruction, which she willfully and recklessly summons. The speaker's fascination with violence (and its relationship to the physical body) is enacted beautifully in Colen's presentation of fire. She writes, for example, in "The Perfect Kind of Happy":

> I hold your hand or I strike you or you strike me or light up a cigarette and our upstairs disappears. But what if we're in it? I think of particles exploding, coming back together like some physics experiment I don't know the name for. "Large Hadron Collider," you say.

Here Colen conflates the act of smoking with interpersonal violence ("I strike you . . . you strike me"), suggesting that this kind of harm is also done slowly and unwittingly to oneself. At the same time, Colen subtly implies that aggression and conflict are built into the very "particles" that make us. For her, this "experiment" represents a necessary destruction, what may be conceived of as a generative kind of violence.

In many ways, the impact of this passage is heightened by repetition on a larger scale, as the small fire portrayed here ("lighting up a cigarette") only grows with each provocative prose piece. Within a few pages, we are presented with "campfire," "an active volcano," and finally, "a face lighting up." The fire that Colen depicts in these passages becomes destruction and resistance, a threat to oneself and the other.

Repetition as Instability and Danger

Salvage by Kristy Bowen offers a provocative take on this framing of repetition as subtle violence, as necessary devastation. We are offered a vision of the self as inherently unstable, a self that is destroyed over and over again, only to emerge more luminous and fierce. What's more, Bowen shows us the speaker's transfiguration frame by frame. This book-length sequence reads as deconstructed cinema, as a gorgeously fractured film reel.

Like Colen and Lerner, Bowen utilizes repetition not only as a source of unity and cohesion, but as metaphor, as an ontological statement. Throughout *Salvage*, voice is born out of the destruction of a self who is not yet past, singing toward a future that has not yet materialized. This Hegelian notion of transformation as destruction, and time as inevitable violence, is perhaps most visible in Bowen's sequence, "dreams about houses and bees." Here the reader is presented with infinite variations on the same image, a house that is at turns "four-chambered" and "falling," that doubles as a "museum of unruly saints." Bowen's use of repetition here is twofold: We are offered a consistent vocabulary of domestic imagery, certainly, but each poem retains a subtle variation on what appears at first to be the same title, with its familiar syntactic construction: "House made of . . ." or "House which is . . ."

Each "house which is a kind of falling," and each "house of misused potential" functions as a projection, a rendering of the speaker's emotional and psychic topography, which is inevitably externalized.

Bowen writes in "house made of ghosts and small animals":

> For every love song, there is a broken dove skeleton
> rotting in the eaves. A leaving, that requires
> nothing but the door opening and closing just once.
> A heaviness of suitcases and floor lamps and
> record albums piled awkwardly in the trunk.

The speaker's interior drama, the "longing" and cruel "motives" that exist simultaneously, are enacted in the objects she chooses to populate the domestic space: "love songs" at odds with "broken dove skeletons," the lightness of music coupled with the "heaviness" of her personal affects. Here, we are presented with a space marked by tension, the speaker's desire for multiple and contradictory outcomes. In many ways, Bowen's rendering of this domestic space is all the more startling, considering the poem immediately before, its rooms populated by "love letters" and "tiny glass kittens."

As the reader wanders the halls of this "house of beautiful drownings," we see a slow transformation of the speaker projected onto the space she inhabits. Through her seamless and artful repetition, Bowen calls our attention to the relationship between time and the rooms we traverse, as each "house of strays," each "house of open wounds," documents a self that is already and irrevocably past. I find myself deeply moved by Bowen's work when she acknowledges temporality as violence, as necessary destruction. In many ways, this repetition, with a slight difference, allows her entry to this ambitious philosophical question.

Salvage is aptly named, as Bowen gracefully and articulately gathers the fragments of each burned house, each broken window. Like Colen and Lerner, Bowen shows us that when we try to hold on to the things we have accumulated—"salt shakers, salad forks, tiny match books"—it's really the space between our fingers that lets the light through.

An earlier version of this essay appeared in the *Literary Review*

Clarification. Or Not.

Jeffrey Levine

I worked with a poet who writes riveting narrative poems, touched with stream-of-consciousness. Nevertheless, when we worked together, they sent me an email that read: "Most places I send this work find it incomprehensible . . . My models for the blank verse are James Merrill's long poems, Robert Frost, and Nabokov's novel, *Pale Fire*. I know these poems don't come up to their standards, so I'd like to improve their quality. I'd also like the narrative clearer so people don't find it so confusing."

I get this a lot from writers chasing the gods of "clarity." I find their work remarkable, and have no problem "following" its engaging turns. Maybe this sentiment is workshop residue, or maybe they're sending the work to the wrong places. Probably both. It's the Apollo on one shoulder, Dionysus on the other thing.

Here's my answer, and what I would say to just about any poet sending out work these days, in the midst of contemporary chaos and a good sixty years after Frost.

First of all, they're wrong. By which I mean, readers who find this work incomprehensible are looking for something you're not doing. Many readers find *Pale Fire* (1962) incomprehensible. Many find *Hamlet* incomprehensible, with all the dithering, baiting, and Freudian undertow. Nearly everyone finds Gertrude Stein to be a certain kind of incomprehensible. Like Nabokov, Shakespeare, Stein, or Emily Dickinson, you embrace a word within a *dreamscape*. Which is where we live, and like our brain, which right-side-ups everything our eyes see, our brains also try to make a certain kind of sense of chaos.

Our job as writers is to capture that chaos and come to some kind of terms with it. As in dreams, not everything adds up, because things don't add up in putative "real life." Order is provisional. As you suggest in your poems. I like when writers give permission to that part of the unconscious that, like the dreamer, lets go of the superego, which is what makes us, in dreaming, psychotic. Something to aim for, that artistic psychosis, without which no Goya or Picasso or Joan Mitchell ("No Birds").

So, my theory of narrative is that we humans need story so badly, we'll manufacture one from the slimmest evidence, whether from the cave walls at Lascaux and Altamira, the papyrus on which a shred of Sappho resides, or that fragment of a letter your mother wrote to your father during the war in which she seemed to be channeling Joyce.

The job of the artist (poet) is to provide just enough to invite the reader in, show the reader around the place, and say some sort of mutually satisfying goodbye. I can give you great exercises for clarifying your narrative, if that's what you're after, as long as you understand that "clarity" is a construct. We have time to do that together with a few of your poems at a Tupelo writing conference, and then you can take it from there. Or, you can rejoice in what you're creating. Or both.

Hybrid Genre Writing: An Introduction

Kristina Marie Darling

This essay is adapted from a course syllabus developed by Kristina Marie Darling.

Figure 1. An Erasure of F. Scott Fitzgerald's *The Great Gatsby*

CHAPTER 3

T hrough the summer nights. men and girls came and went like moths and the stars. I watched his guests slit the waters of the Sound, the city scampered like a brisk yellow bug eight servants, left his back door in a pyramid of pulpless halves.

At least enough colored lights to make a Christmas tree bewitched to a dark gold. so long forgotten

Here is F. Scott Fitzgerald's masterpiece, erased, blacked out by a reader's magic marker. She has kept what is useful to her, and done away with the rest. Some might call this gesture irreverent, disrespectful, or even destructive. But writers do the same thing every day. When crafting a story or a poem, one selects the elements of convention that are useful, discarding the rest. Every poem, every story, and every essay is a deconstruction (and revision, and erasure) of the work that came before it. We select the parts of convention we wish to preserve, and there's nothing disrespectful about it; this is merely the writer's job.

In my opinion, this erasure is useful for thinking about hybrid genre work for several reasons. First of all, you are selecting the aspects of genre convention that you wish to work with, and blacking out the rest. And even when working in hybrid forms, genre is still present, in much the same way that Fitzgerald's text is still visible beneath the black markings of the erasure. For example, when we see a short story, we expect a certain type of narrative arc. For the writer, these readerly expectations are material, knowledge you can use to surprise the reader and make them think. This is one of the primary goals of hybrid writing. Even when working in the most experimental modes, the ghosts of tradition, literary history, and genre convention will haunt your work. Just as the reader of the text shown above expected a pristine, unbroken narrative, your readers will come to your hybrid work with preconceived ideas about how stories unfold. I will present some exercises that will help you work on using these readerly expectations to your advantage, making readers think, showing them new possibilities within received forms, and fostering more open-minded reading practices. Like the individual who erased Gatsby, in your hybrid work you will select only the elements of tradition that are useful to you, forgetting the rest, or better yet, inventing the rest.

Hybrid Genre Writing: A Spectrum

Before we can work on manipulating the reader's expectations, let's consider the broad range of types of experimental writing being published today. Hybrid work can have elements of poetry, nonfiction, scholarship, fiction, or any combination thereof. Here's a breakdown of how the traditional genres overlap and intersect.

In the diagram shown above, several traditional genre categories (fiction, poetry, creative nonfiction, and formal academic writing) are shown in black cells. Hybrid genres are shown in white cells. What does the term hybrid mean, exactly? For the purposes of this essay, hybrid writing is any type of literary work that utilizes the resources of more than one traditional genre category. Here are some definitions and representative authors that illustrate the range of hybrid genre work that exists in today's literary landscape.

Lyrical Fiction: This term often refers to fiction (in novel or story form) that draws from the stylistic repertoire of poetry. Fiction that uses alliteration, assonance, consonance, and the repetition of sounds more generally, to create meaning. Fiction that relies on recurring imagistic motifs for structure and coherence, rather than narrative in the traditional sense. Lyric prose frequently uses these poetic devices to heighten narrative suspense, and to elicit even more of an emotional response from the reader than the narrative itself could. The techniques of poetry supplement, create, and drive narrative in lyrical fiction. If you're looking for some enjoyable examples available online, Carol Guess, Joanna Penn Cooper, Kelly Magee, Matt Bell, and Molly Gaudry are a few well-known contemporary authors working in this field.

Lyric Essay: This term frequently refers to creative nonfiction that draws from the resources of poetry. Lyric essays, like creative nonfiction, draw their inspiration from the events of real life. But, like lyrical fiction, they frequently use the stylistic devices of poetry to elicit an emotional response from the reader. The lyric essay tradition is rich with imagistic motifs, fragmentation, and recursive narrative structures. The story folds in on itself, returning to images, ideas, and language from earlier in the text, often in a different context. Much like poetry, the lyric essay takes the imagery surrounding an experience (think of everyday objects, love tokens, mementos), then inscribes it and reinscribes it with myriad possibilities for interpretation. Meaning accumulates, gathering around the detritus of a past experience. Unlike conventional prose works, which have a linear structure, lyric essays will circle around the same object or experience, which gains significance with each tangential orbit. Some contemporary practitioners of lyric essay include Maggie Nelson, Julie Marie Wade, and Eula Biss. If you're interested, all three writers have work freely available online.

Creative Literary Criticism: There's a great deal of hybrid genre work that questions the boundaries between "critical" and "creative" writing. These distinctions can be seen as arbitrary, and they reflect larger power structures within the literary community and in the academy. Those in power decide what can be counted as "scholarship." Perhaps the best-known example of this type of writing is Jenny Boully's *The Body: An Essay* (Essay Press, 2007). In this collection, Boully takes an academic form of writing (footnotes) and fills it with content that doesn't seem academic at first glance: personal narratives, aestheticized language, and even descriptions of dreams. By using form in such a way, Boully calls our attention to the artificiality of the categories we impose upon language. Indeed, personal experience, beauty, and the unconscious mind can all be brought to bear on theoretical debates. Other practitioners of creative scholarship include Kristy Bowen, Thalia Field, Spring Ulmer, and Carla Harryman.

Suggested Readings: Types of Hybridity

Lyrical Fiction

G. C. Waldrep, "Stigmatic Affection" (*Cordite Poetry Review*):_http://cordite.org.au/poetry/whitehomes/stigmatic-affection/

Richard Siken, "War of the Foxes" (*Cordite Poetry Review*): http://cordite.org.au/poetry/whitehomes/war-of-the-foxes-ii/

Matt Bell, "The Girl in the Golden Hood" (*NANO Fiction*): http://nanofiction.org/weekly-feature/featured-story/2014/05/the-girl-in-the-golden-hood

Lyric Essay

Eula Biss, "The Balloonists" (https://eulabiss.net/excerpt-balloonists.html)

Creative Literary Criticism

Kristy Bowen, "algorithms" and "footnotes to a history of desire" (*Alice Blue Review*): http://www.alicebluereview.org/four/poetry/bowen.html

Exercising Hybridity

The following exercise is designed to get you thinking about hybridizing genres in your own writing.

Erasing (or Inventing) Genre. Choose a form of writing that's decidedly "uncreative." This can be anything, from an advertisement to a footnote. Here are a few possibilities:

- Footnotes to a book or article
- A glossary
- Endnotes
- An appendix
- Job listing
- Job application letter
- Conference presentation

- Abstract for a scholarly paper
- An encyclopedia entry
- An advertisement
- An etiquette guidebook
- A travel guide

Pick anything that interests you, but it should be a form of writing that readers expect to be practical—a type of writing that usually does its job, nothing less, nothing more.

After you've chosen your form, make a list of elements that a reader will expect to find. For example, if you're writing a "job application letter," you know a reader would expect to find a list of credentials, an applicant's name, his or her contact information, and perhaps some information on how the writer meets the qualifications of the job. After you've considered the components of this type of writing, decide which ones to keep, and choose which ones to discard. For the job application letter, you might keep the letter format, but not include the applicant's credentials. Once some of the elements of the genre have been discarded, think about what you will put in their place. Insert an unexpected element into this practical form of writing, whether it's content, sound, imagery, fragmentation, unconventional grammar, etc. Consider carefully what the reader will expect, and what they won't expect. How can you use what's familiar to surprise them?

A great example is Robert Miltner's "Hope is a Feathered Thing," http://www.leahbrowning.net/Apple/Fall_2007/Robert_Miltner.html.

Publishing Hybrid Genre Work in Literary Magazines: A Taxonomy

One thing writers tend to forget is that literary magazines are almost always edited by writers. In many cases, they're just as deeply invested in subverting genre categories as we are. Just because your work doesn't fall neatly into one of the submission categories (which are almost always cut and dry: poetry, fiction, nonfiction, book reviews, etc.), don't think you won't be published. It's simply a matter of finding the literary editors who read in a like-minded way.

Look again at the genre spectrum illustrated above. There are magazines that fall on opposite ends of this spectrum, and everywhere in between. Additionally, this interest in hybrid genre work frequently isn't reflected in the available submission categories. Here's a comprehensive list of magazines that are deeply invested in interrogating genre categories. Even websites that are no longer actively taking submissions are treasure troves of contemporary hybrid or experimental writing.

Lyrical Fiction and Prose Poetry

100 Word Story: www.100wordstory.org/
111O: miel.ohbara.com/wordpress/our-journal-111o/
3AM Magazine: www.3ammagazine.com/3am/
HOOT Review: www.hootreview.com/
Monkeybicycle: monkeybicycle.net/
Plume magazine: plumepoetry.com/
The Prick of the Spindle: www.prickofthespindle.com/
The Prose Poem: An International Journal: webdelsol.com/tpp/
Smokelong Quarterly: www.smokelong.com/
Tarpaulin Sky magazine: www.tarpaulinsky.com/magazine/
Vestal Review: www.vestalreview.net/

Lyric Essay

Black Warrior Review: bwr.ua.edu/
Brevity: brevitymag.com/
CutBank Magazine: www.cutbankonline.org/
Denver Quarterly: www.du.edu/denverquarterly/
Fourth Genre: fourthgenre.byu.edu/
Fugue: fuguejournal.com/
Hippocampus Magazine: www.hippocampusmagazine.com/
Matter: A Journal of Compressed Creative Arts: matterpress.com

Mid-American Review: casit.bgsu.edu/midamericanreview/
Narrative Magazine: www.narrativemagazine.com/
River Teeth: A Journal of Nonfiction Narrative:
www.riverteethjournal.com/
Seneca Review: https://www.hws.edu/senecareview/
TriQuarterly Online: www.triquarterly.org/

Creative Literary Criticism
Alice Blue Review: www.alicebluereview.org/
A Public Space: apublicspace.org/
The Constant Critic: http://fencedigital.com/fence-digital/constant-critic/
DIAGRAM: www.thediagram.com/
Eratio: www.eratiopostmodernpoetry.com
Gone Lawn: journal.gonelawn.net
Word For/Word: www.wordforword.info

This list of markets is only the beginning. It demonstrates that there's a home for almost every literary text, however avant-garde or genre bending.

Building from the Ground Up: Writing the Hybrid-Form Manuscript

Katie Farris

Form Shapes Idea

Although most readers are more focused on the *content* of a book—its characters, plot, or argument—than on its *form*, literary forms have evolved, or been constructed to be "containers" for specific types of information. Think—it would be impossible to show the complexities and contradictions of Toni Morrison's character Beloved in a three-line haiku. Likewise, Robert Bly's translation of Basho's haiku—"The temple bell stops / but the sound keeps coming / out of the flowers"—is a complete artistic gesture in thirteen words, something a novel couldn't accomplish. No matter how brilliant a book's content, if its form isn't reflective of its ideas, it won't be a durable work of literature, because it isn't teaching its reader to think in a new way.

Hybrid-form books invent themselves anew; they defy our conventional expectations of literary form, and therefore, the ways we're used to thinking. In other words: As readers, we're often well-prepared to think *about* something in a new light, but we're rarely prepared to question *how* we think—how our thoughts are constructed, how we expect information to be ordered or presented, and ultimately, how we choose to order and present what we know. Hybrid-form books are constructed to challenge their readers to reinvent the way they think.

Audre Lorde's maxim, "The master's tools will never dismantle the master's house," resonates strongly with the creation of the hybrid-form text: built from necessity, from the ground up, using a collage of different techniques over many different genres. Constructing an entirely new form, hybrid texts give their author the ability to tell stories never told before, to articulate ideas never articulated before, and to relate experiences never related before.

Perhaps it's no surprise, then, that so many of the book-length hybrid works that have changed literature, especially in the last century, have been written by people of color. There are many, but to list a few: *The Revenge of the Moon-Cake Vixen* by Marilyn Chin (W. W. Norton, 2009), *Maud Martha* by Gwendolyn Brooks (1953), *The Way to Rainy Mountain* by N. Scott Momaday (1969), *Cane* by Jean Toomer (1923), *Dictee* by Theresa Hak-Kyung Cha (Tanam Press, 1982), and *The House on Mango Street* by Sandra Cisneros (Arte Publico Press, 1984).

As authors, one of the great pleasures of learning about the construction of hybrid forms is that we learn how to ask more effective questions of all forms, and therefore, all of literature. Below, I'll examine three works in the impossible canon of hybrid-form literature, looking at how each author uses unusual formal choices to reinvent the way we think.

The Way to Rainy Mountain

N. Scott Momaday's *The Way to Rainy Mountain* layers lineated poetry, essays, line drawings, and a three-paragraph form of his own invention to tell the story of two hundred years of the history of the Kiowa people. As with many hybrid texts, the book's structure is so unusual that we're forced to meet it on its own terms, relying on the text, rather than previous experience, to teach us how to read it. Momaday makes the contract between reader and writer explicit with a lot of front matter: a poem, a prologue, and an introduction. In his prologue, he presents the book as a journey:

> The journey herein recalled continues to be made anew each time the miracle comes to mind. . . . [I]t is made with the whole memory, that experience of the mind which is legendary as well as historical, personal, as well as cultural. . . . The imaginative experience and

> the historical express equally the traditions of man's reality.

With this intention laid out, the reader can move into the meat of the book with more confidence, this passage echoing as an answer to many of the questions we might ask as we move through the text.

The main portion of the book is composed of a two-page form of Momaday's invention; each spread, which typically explores a theme, comprises three paragraphs, reflecting the list from his preface above: the first is the Kiowa cultural voice, stories passed down orally for generations. The second paragraph is a historical insight, and the third is Momaday's personal experience, a sort of memoir related as poetic prose.

As the book progresses, something unexpected begins to happen: Momaday's grandfather, Mammedaty, journeys from the personal sections into the historical sections. Eventually, he migrates into the Kiowa oral tradition. The neat and tidy categories that Momaday constructed toward the beginning of the book begin to dissolve as Mammedaty walks all over them. This could initially frustrate the reader, as Momaday seems to violate his own rules. But as we question *why* this formal choice has been made, the reader begins to think differently, asking ourselves why must these genres be separate at all? Don't our individual lives engage, after all, with the historic and even the mythic? Can history not be personal? Where is that intriguing place where the stories our ancestors tell meet history? How can one distinguish one's own history from that of one's community?

Momaday is a distinguished man of letters; he could have told this story as a fine novel, or as a memoir. But arguably, memoirs and novels aren't sufficient to these questions, particularly the last. After all, they are forms *born* from capitalism and individualism, and born in the same moment society began to tell itself that a person (almost always a man) was, must be, independent of all others. There wasn't a form of literature that could hold, with equal importance, the imaginative and historical experience of humanity. So Momaday made one up, and taught us how to think anew.

Dictee

Like *The Way to Rainy Mountain,* Teresa Hak Kyung Cha's *Dictee* is another hybrid-form text that reckons with the idea of autobiography in the context of colonial history. In this case, Cha sets her own experiences, particularly those of learning and using language, alongside the experiences of her mother in Korea, and the broader history of Koreans, especially the Korean revolutionary Yu Guan Soon, under Japan's brutal colonial rule. The book particularly delves into the experience of the colonized tongue, of language as a colonial tool. A hybrid form is uniquely suited to this kind of complex question: How can one use language (and in Cha's chase, image) to show the complexities of how language controls our thinking, culture, and lives? *How can one build a text that resists that control?*

Dictee subverts readerly expectations of the "novel" (as the book is called) at every turn. Among other inventive techniques, Cha refuses all but the barest hints of narrative; she passes from one language into another, almost always without translation. She interrupts text with photographs, diagrams, letters, graffiti, and other images. She uses white space in innovative ways, often creating conundrums of how to read two facing leaves: top to bottom, left to right, or perhaps top-to-bottom across both leaves? Or alternating across leaves?

Even in the single superficial way that the book appears like a novel, through its division into nine sections or chapters, each named after one of the Greek muses, Cha wittily and quietly replaces the muse of music, Euterpe, with a muse of her own invention, "Elitere," a nonsense name without basis in Greek or Latin that nevertheless seems to evoke the idea of literacy itself.

Unlike *The Way to Rainy Mountain* and many other hybrid texts, neither Cha nor her publishers provide an introduction, creating a much more challenging experience for the first-time reader, especially one unfamiliar with the wide variety of historical and cultural references Cha uses, whether to film direction, Korean history, or French elementary-school practices. Entering into *Dictee* can feel like entering an entirely new nation speaking a dialect of our language; understandable in its broadest strokes but bewildering in its rhetorical moves.

Arguably, any book is a subjective experience, created as a partnership between writer and reader. *Dictee* emphasizes this experience through many techniques, especially Cha's usage of many languages. Therefore, interpretation of the text can function in multiple interesting ways, depending on the reader's linguistic abilities. For example, four massive Chinese characters, each taking up an entire page, are interspersed through the book. Some readers will simply read them as part of the larger text: "Woman," "Man," "Father," "Mother." For those illiterate in Chinese, they can be thought of as a decorative motif, an obstacle to moving forward, an opportunity to learn, a sign of Otherness, or any number of other interpretations.

At every turn, Cha actively resists controlling the reader's interpretation of the text, allowing the reader to meet it on their own terms. It's a sort of decolonization of the reading experience, an entirely new way of approaching a piece of literature. To what end? That question has a thousand answers in the book, but one of the most powerful, perhaps, is from the first section, "Clio/History":

> Why resurrect it all now. From the Past. History, the old wound. The past emotions all over again. To confess to relive the same folly. To name it now so as not to repeat history in oblivion. To extract each fragment by each fragment from the word from the image another word another image the reply that will not repeat history in oblivion.

In *Dictee*, Cha pushes back against traditional forms and ideas of what a text could or must be; it unpeels colonial structures, inventing its own language and rhetorical structure even as it uses classical references, only to later burn those bridges with wit.

Invisible Cities and Outro

As we have seen, hybrid texts can be an extraordinary space for telling stories that have been historically and actively suppressed and ignored; stories that complicate ideas of the individual in ways that the Western white cisheteropatriarchy would prefer to simplify into stories of men leaving their rags behind for riches. Interestingly, hybrid forms seem to provide a productive space to step outside of received knowledge and into the realm of speculative thought for those who do live in the center of culture; to imagine that the world is, or could be, another way.

Italo Calvino's *Invisible Cities* (1972) is another hybrid-form book labelled a "novel," though like *Dictee*, it has only the barest of narrative momentum. Written in Italy, the book is reckoning with a different history than *Dictee* or *The Way to Rainy Mountain*, though colonialism is still at its core. The book opens with Kublai Khan meditating on the idea of empire:

> In the lives of emperors there is a moment which follows pride in the boundless extension of the territories we have conquered, and the melancholy and relief of knowing we shall soon give up any thought of knowing and understanding them . . . It is the desperate moment when we discover that this empire, which had seemed to us the sum of all wonders, is an endless, formless ruin, that corruption's gangrene has spread too far to be healed by our scepter, that the triumph over enemy sovereigns has made us the heirs of their long undoing.

Khan, and therefore the text, is preoccupied with how one might find direction or meaning at the center of an unimaginably vast and diverse empire. He feels inherently alienated; as Calvino puts it, "the emperor is he who is a foreigner to each of his subjects, and only through foreign eyes and ears could the empire manifest its existence to Kublai." The only time he feels something like a pattern is when the explorer Marco Polo tells him stories of various cities throughout the empire.

Invisible Cities explores whether it's possible to communicate across languages, class, and culture, and whether any two people can ever look at the same city, word, or symbol and come to some agreement about its meaning. Therefore, Calvino seems to be calling into question *everything* we must agree upon to read or write a traditional text. He, like Cha, tries to build a text that resists control—not just of language, but of meaning itself. And once again, it is hard to imagine anything but a hybrid-form text capable of exploring the questions he presents.

Formally, what's perhaps most striking about the book as a hybrid text is how it seems to enact a series of erasures: Each of the fifty-five chapters is a description of a new city, but they never build upon one another. Each new chapter seems to begin the book again, reinventing the world anew, over and over. Even the one thread of narrative, short discussions between Polo and Khan interspersed mathematically between chapters, never creates a sense of plot or forward momentum; each one repetitively wonders whether an empire is ever graspable from the perspective of the emperor, ever describable from the perspective of the explorer.

In these dialogues, the possibility of communication itself is called into question. Polo sometimes mimes his stories, sometimes arranges objects in a series of relationships "like chessmen," sometimes tells the stories in perfect Tartar; sometimes Khan describes a city, demanding Polo go out and find it; sometimes Polo sits silently, presumably grokking the information directly into the grand imperial brain. Time itself is unreliable: One dialogue might take place only to have the next rewound by several years, before Polo was able to speak in the Tartar language. As you might imagine, the repetitiveness of the city descriptions (as delightful as they are!) and the strange, dreamy, repetitive conversations between Khan and Polo can be frustrating to anyone expecting the forward momentum of a novel.

Midway through the book, Polo reveals that each of the cities is perhaps the city of Venice, seeming to emphasize the absurdity of the empire, perhaps of imperialism itself. If one city has so many faces, why bother collecting a continent's worth?

This idea of the singular city, the city that preempts all others, is one that Calvino returns to at the end of the text. Khan wonders aloud about the point of exploration or empire building, if one is heading only toward death, which Calvino fashions as the "infernal city." Marco Polo responds:

> The inferno of the living is not something that will be; if there is one, it is what is already here, the inferno where we live every day, that we form by being together. There are two ways to escape suffering it. The first is easy for many; accept the inferno and become such a part of it that you can no longer see it. The second is risky and demands constant vigilance and apprehension: seek and learn to recognize who and what, in the midst of inferno, are not inferno, then make them endure, give them space.

It seems to me that this is what each of these texts is attempting to do: to find, whether at the locus or the margins of an alienating culture, that which stands against or defies not only the *content* of that culture, but the *forms* it uses to convey that culture; to find what isn't inferno and give it space.

Hybrid forms resist by subverting the idea that the reality we're always served is the only reality. They imagine a different world, or show us new ways to think about and experience the world as it is. Hybrid forms give us new ways to think and engage; they are specialty tools like the aye-aye's crazy-long finger, formed to pull insect larva out of tree bark. They are investigative forms, revolutionary forms. They nourish what is strange in us.

"Almost Everyone Was Mistaken": On Secrets, Light, and the Lyric Imagination

Kristina Marie Darling

In his recent essay collection, Peter Balakian defines "shadow" as a "force that follows something with fidelity" only to "cast a dark light" on that person, object, view, or perspective. (*Vise and Shadow*, University of Chicago Press, 2015). For Balakian, this fraught proximity—a closeness that blocks the line of vision—is one of the most essential characteristics of a work of art. After all, it is what we sense, but do not yet see, that beckons us farther into a half-lit room. The careful architecture of a poem—a space that is gradually illuminated for the reader—depends upon all that is hidden as a necessary condition, much more so than on the visible beauty or significance of a particular image.

Three recent hybrid works fully do justice to this intricate relationship between secrets, shadow, and the aesthetic imagination. In Henry Hoke's *Genevieves* (Subito Press, 2017), Kirsten Kaschock's *Confessional Sci-Fi: A Primer* (Subito Press, 2017), and Matthew Rohrer's *The Others* (Wave Books, 2017), the unknown emerges as a source of both light and its surrounding darkness. Though vastly different in style and approach, these three writers share a gift for a skillful and calculated withholding, the suggestion of a buried narrative "quietly ghosting" all that is immediately perceptible. Here, what is hidden offers an invitation, an occasion for collaboration between the poem and its reader, creating a third space that belongs to both of them (and at the same time, neither of them). Each of these texts becomes "a glass bridge between buildings," the beginning of an incandescent structure that is built across temporal, psychic, and geographic boundaries.

Early in the twentieth century, modernists described this kind of innovative text as a "machine for generating meaning." The poet's task, then, was to guide the reader's imaginative work, slowly revealing a vast and luminous fictive terrain without limiting what is possible within it. In the work of Hoke, Kaschock, and Rohrer this graceful movement between revelation and concealment is most visible in their treatment of familiar narrative structures. We are uncertain whether the "pursuit" is ending or beginning, as the reader almost always finds herself "where it all began." "You will wonder if it was the threshold," Kaschock explains. In each of these beautifully rendered collections, uncertainty becomes a "window," an "entrance," and an "invention."

Genevieves

Henry Hoke's *Genevieves* reads as a ledger of what cannot, will not, be said aloud. Presented as a series of intricately linked hybrid texts, which are each themselves composed of discrete episodes, Hoke's writing allows uncertainty to accumulate in the space between things. These absences, the "silent" and "unsmiling" gaps between prose narratives, articulate—through their expertly timed jump cuts and ruptures—a question that is refined over the course of the larger collection. In this subtle and beguiling book, Hoke asks what happens when we refuse to speak, whether this refusal constitutes an end

> —to discovery, knowledge, and self-actualization—or possibility, a beautiful "doorway" opening "with a flourish."

Reminiscent of early twentieth-century experimental films, particularly their creators' predilection for montage, Hoke reminds us that silence, and the subsequent lack of a clear narrative, make space for the other, inviting "the Crowd" in all of its problematic splendor into the room. He writes, for example, in the first section of this haunted and haunting collection:

> Weaponize your juvenilia.
>
> There are only so many times you can come home before you have to decide why you're there. Before you have to decide when you're getting away. Carolina sat.
>
> There was a soft cough outside her door. Carolina opened it with a crack and met her half-brother for the first time.
>
> I've also been hiding, he said.

Hoke offers a seamless matching of style and content, as the preponderance of secrets in this Southern family is enacted within the behavior of the language itself. Here, the connections between things, the transitional language we are so accustomed to, is purposefully admitted. For example, each sentence, and the widening expanses between them, asks of the reader a leap in logic, point of view, and syntax. This movement between perspectives is perhaps most visible when the speaker's half-brother walks through the door ("I've also been hiding"). Like a room opening inside what we thought was a single room, the narrative generates possibility through these abrupt shifts in rhetorical modes, and the line of reasoning that each one represents. As Hoke's prose ambulates between ways of seeing, and the elisions they give rise to, we are prompted—inevitably, irrefutably—to locate ourselves in this gorgeously imagined topography. Hoke himself explains, "As I slip below the waves I'll see light."

Confessional Sci-Fi

Kirsten Kaschock's *Confessional Sci-Fi: A Primer* continues this engagement with concealment and its seemingly infinite possibilities for readerly participation. Here, too, the transitional language we have come to expect is skillfully hidden from view. We are offered a montage "brimming with chocolates," "cigarettes," and "dipped carnations," all stripped of their narrative artifice, that unnecessary ornamentation. Similar in structure to *Genevieves*, Kaschock's discrete prose texts represent a dialogue between facets of the same voice, or parts of the same consciousness, rather than a conventionally unified narrative. Her elliptical and gorgeously fractured texts—and the echoing space between them—also becomes metaphor, instructing us as to how the work should be read, engaged with, and imagined with.

For Kaschock, all of thought is a conversation, evoking what Mikhail Bakhtin described as "the dialogic imagination." Just as she responds to and interrogates her own observations, deconstructing the various ways of seeing that she inhabits, Kaschock prompts her reader to do the same. Consider the transition between sections in "After Museum":

> To the museum's visitors (a collective to which you now belong)
>
> the two-way guide is a winged primate, atrophying.
>
> ---
>
> The first room is one woman. A strung-out. She is laid on a loom, and her eyes have accepted this.

Kaschock's presentation of the "woman" reads as a response to the images of community that are presented in the first stanza—that "collective to which you now belong." As the poem unfolds, she refines these recurring questions of choice and agency, considering our roles as readers and consumers of mass culture. More specifically, the text posits the human mind as a museum, exhibiting the various ephemera, cultural symbols, and pieces of language that have accumulated within it—mementoes that we have not necessarily chosen ourselves. As "the museum's visitors" wander Kaschock's display of elusive, elliptical hybrid creations, they become themselves curators, and Kaschock is implicated in her own incisive, thought-provoking cultural critique. Yet the moment we think we have discerned intent, "it all flies outside and into the porchlight like moths, of course and forever."

The Others

Wonderfully ambitious and fully realized, Matthew Rohrer's *The Others* engages similar questions of readerly participation and, more specifically, the cultivation of a shared consciousness through art. In the book's sprawling fictive terrain, the constant presence of the other within the self—that eternal alterity—is a shadow story that haunts the narrative proper. As the work unfolds, it is this secret, hidden most of all from the speaker of the poem, that is gradually revealed, understood, and dramatized beautifully in the style of the writing itself.

Early in the poem, Rohrer's speaker makes frequent reference to "the others," speculating about their inner lives. "At least I always assumed the others hated their jobs too," he writes. Here, and elsewhere in the opening pages, we encounter a clear divide between subject and object that is skillfully interrogated, and incisively deconstructed, as the book unfolds. Indeed, the polyphonic, collectively voiced style of the poem complicates this line of thinking, positing all of thought, and our life in language, as a shared endeavor. The project often takes the form of a linguistic collage, a carefully orchestrated assemblage of attributed language. For example, he writes,

> "It wasn't real, I think,

but I saw it for sure.
The image was broadcast
To my brain to see it.
So I saw it, I guess.

"Well, that's not really much

of a ghost story, Ron.
I've actually got one.
Can I tell it to you?"

In much the same way that the story takes up haunting as one of its primary considerations, we are made to see voice as persistently inhabited by language and rhetoric that is not one's own. This idea manifests perhaps most visibly in Rohrer's use of dialogue. This passage, like many others in the collection, transitions swiftly between quoted sections, the narrative arising from what is really a chorus of voices, a vocal and dissonant collective. With that in mind, his technique not only becomes commentary on the narrative, it becomes the narrative. This provocative tension—between what is explicitly stated and all that is implied by the behavior of the language itself—is what drives the collection. What's more, this disconnect, this gorgeous complexity, becomes an aperture, a doorway through which the reader may enter the work's vast and radiant fictive topography.

Much like Hoke and Kaschock, Rohrer purposefully refuses exposition, bringing to mind Objectivist poets like Oppen, Niedecker, and Zukofsky. Yet *The Others* situates this rich artistic tradition in a dialogue with more recent conceptual writing and the lyric, ultimately refining the Objectivists' initial question, that lingering doubt as to whether the aesthetic imagination can exist in isolation. Rohrer shows us that voice arises within the context of a community, and that we are indebted to it, whether or not we fully realize it. As Rohrer himself reminds us, "the gate is already down / and the trap has been sprung."

On the Idea of Order: A Western Key

Jeffrey Levine

All criticism is an argument, of course, and critique by one writer of another is the urging of a particular worldview. Curtis Faville, who writes a blog, "The Compass Rose," has written this rather energetic critique of the advice I offered in "The Poetry Manuscript: Arts and Crafts":

> If the book is, in whole, as you quote Frost as claiming, itself a "poem" then it should be subject to the same requirements as any art-form. If your conception of the "book" is a traditional form established over time, what's implied is that it's an enormous cliché, which is like a metaphorical quotation of something already done. Creative thinking, and writing, and book-making, demand that we re-think the form every time we indulge in it. Your whole list is like a recipe for a completely predictable, dull book. Which is pretty much what we have in the poetry world. Have you checked the poetry shelves, lately? Fully 97% of all you find is instantly forgettable, in large measure because of the common acceptance of the formula you offer here.

Faville's argument (based upon many readings of Curtis' reviews, blog, and this comment) is for something new in the poetry world. Something that transcends the ordinary and, therefore, the previous. I would argue that I'm also fighting for that. Which makes me wonder whether my advice does, as he suggests, rule out the creation of something new: new ways of seeing a poem, new ways of seeing a book.

It's interesting to think about those early, fervent urgings of Whitman for something new in poetry, and later, a perhaps derivative, but no less memorable philosophy of William Carlos Williams. Each argued for the new: for the shattering of molds. For a way, or ways, a poem might sound that sounds nothing like it sounded before. But it seems important to add here that Williams and Whitman wanted innovation rooted in intentional, disciplined decision making.

There's Whitman writing (and writing) to Emerson about "Individuality, that new moral American contine" (*Leaves of Grass*, 2nd edition). There's Williams, one of "The Others," those early American modernists, gobbling up Joyce and Duchamp, Man Ray, H. D., and of course getting his pounds' worth from Pound's edict to "make it new."

But let's get back to the essential question of how to make a book of poetry out of a batch of poems (and let's sort of accept that anything memorable—anything worth reading—must in some ineluctable sense be "new"). I have urged taking various ways of looking at order, of ordering a manuscript, as useful in generating new ways of looking at the poems themselves—revising, sure, but also *revisioning*. What does a poem want to mean? What discoveries does it want to make? What techniques might prepare the poem to set off on this course of discovery?

I think it is worthwhile to consider how we think about the question of what goes with what. What sorts of decisions do art gallery curators make—and how do they make them—when hanging a show? Obviously, there are shows that cry out for an "easy" sort of order: chronological, or oils with oils, charcoal with charcoal, and so on. But suppose you're hanging an exhibit of Fauvists and you have fifty pictures by a good half-dozen painters. What sorts of aesthetic decisions are involved?

Contemporary culture is filled with guides to figuring out which of this order of things goes with what of that order of stuff. Which herbs and spices go with that food? It's a useful cognate when you think about it, as (obviously) each herb and each spice added to a particular food changes that food, and by consequence, what it tastes like, and by consequence, what it goes with. If a chef is paying attention, or you in your own kitchen, you are reinventing your recipes as you add and subtract, keep your notes, taste this and try that. If you're blessed with a really good palate, you might even come up with something wholly new, even something memorable.

The same goes for wines (or shoes, ties, or lipstick shades). What wine with what food? Different foods will make different wines taste different. You can find wine-pairing tables all over the place, but here's something I chanced upon the other day: fabulous tables of food pairings. For example, do you need to know which foods go best with Peruvian chocolate (who doesn't)? Somebody has given a LOT of thought to Peruvian dark chocolate. Was there a Platonic ideal to consult? Is there one now?

Think about how classical piano recitals are often organized (or "programmed") chronologically. You get your Scarlatti, then your Mozart, after that your Schubert, later maybe a little Chopin. Why? Is this the Platonic ideal? Well, then, it turns out that I do have an argument.

Poets write to me, despairingly, "but there are so many possible orders for a poetry manuscript!" Of course there are. But, before you settle on a suitable order, the key to creating a memorable book is to take the matter of creating order as an opportunity to look much more closely at your poems.

Along those lines, as you lay your poems side by side by side, here are some questions you might want to ask of each and every poem with respect to the ones alongside it. In what way or ways does that poem (the one under the spotlight):

- deepen
- open up
- interrogate the premises of
- expand upon
- enlarge upon
- focus down on specifics of
- decorate
- glaze
- gloss
- experiment with

- innovate from

the poems it abuts, and the ones by the door, and the one that's nearly under the rug.

What we want—you, me, the editors who read your newly submitted manuscript, Curtis Faville when he reviews your book, and most important, your readers—is, without any argument, something wholly memorable. Whether that means that it must be post-avant in feel or must instead pay consistent homage to the received traditions, two notions seem certain:

1. How you create your poems and the way you form the book itself will need to be rooted in intentional, disciplined decision making (even if those disciplined choices lead to something wholly serendipitous).
2. You won't get there by treating the poems as made things, gods at a feast, ready for prime time, unless you understand what I've been urging: the litany of manuscript-making tools offers an essential scaffolding for further discovery.

What My Mother Taught Me: Practical and Impractical Advice for the Poet on the Making of a Poetry Manuscript

Lise Goett

A long time ago, my mother decided to dispense with convention and live to suit herself. She did this, I think, with a certain amount of panache; and in general, I find myself drawn to people who have the strength of character to do this in art as well as in life. Picasso did this. Gertrude Stein did this. "Fifty million Frenchmen can't be wrong" was a slogan popularized in a Sophie Tucker song during Prohibition.[1] "They *can* be wrong," my mother would say. "They can be wrong for you." At a certain point it's no longer relevant to me whether art pleases. Whether a poem successfully incarnates a vision, and whether that vision is worth having, is what's important to me.

Write the book, you, yourself, want to exist. Nothing else. Voltaire was right: "The best is the enemy of the good."[2] Dare to be great.

Poems that take the path of least critical resistance may enjoy great popularity during a poet's lifetime, but in the scheme of things, be doomed because, out of the desire to please, the poem may lack the very thing distinguished enough to resist the erosion of Time. Remember the liquefaction of Julia's clothes.[3] Would Whitman have survived in Longfellow's workshop? Conversely, there must be something in you, in every poem, which is so convicted that you would not change it for anyone. You know where these places are; and you know the poems that lack these places entirely. The world contains enough mediocre poems already. Why does it need one more?

To be a poet one must have the spirit of an Iditarod husky. You must have the spirit, the heart, to pull even when others have said *that's enough exertion, that's good enough*. You must want something from yourself, an excellence, beyond what anyone would ever ask of you. Your great fear must be that you are not capable of doing this, but you persevere, doggedly, in spite of this fear, and in the face of it. It is the hardest work that we do as poets: to face the wave of the page, of the self, head-on.

Take it from Franz Kafka:

> The kinds of books that make us happy are the kind we could write ourselves if we had to. But we need the books that affect us like a disaster, that grieve us deeply, like the death of someone we loved more than ourselves, like being banished into forests far from everyone, like a suicide. A book must be the axe for the frozen sea inside us. That is my belief.
>
> —Franz Kafka, in a letter to Oskar Pollak[4]

We seem to have drifted far from Kafka's perspective to an adage of marketing. Poetry has become a commodity like everything else. Within the first seven seconds of meeting, people will have a solid impression of who you are—and some research suggests a tenth of a second is all it takes to start determining traits like trustworthiness. Publishers are no different. Despite the $28 you've spent on an entry fee and a promise to read every single manuscript cover to cover, a screener/publisher/reader/janitorial service faced with 1,200-2,000 manuscripts from which to pick one or two for publication is going to have an impression about whether to put you in a pile for further consideration in the first ten minutes of examination.

Poets are notorious narcissists. No publisher of poetry is in it for the monetary reward. They are supporting the publication of poetry as if it were an endangered species or genre. But how do you, Franz Kafka, survive the odds? I've counseled hundreds of clients on the art of arranging a winning manuscript, and this is what I have to say on the subject.

The Power of Three

In the Orthodox tradition of icon writing, the icon writer "casts" the raw pigments onto the panel. This stage represents the chaos of creation, the element of raw potential contained in this mixing together of elements. This chaos is fertile, essential, but no one can live in chaos forever. Eventually, the ego reasserts itself. The lines represent the boundaries of the ego. Just as human consciousness emerges from chaos (a nervous breakdown, the loss of a loved one, the death of our natural environment), a sense of self and individuality emerges. In this stage, the first glimpse of the form that the new cycle is taking, either in a single poem or manuscript, emerges. In the icon-writing process, this casting on and drawing off of new pigment takes place three times. It is only in the last stage of the process that the finish is applied, and the icon is blessed with oil and the image sealed. Icon writers believe that the image is alive and has its own work to do in the world, like a child that leaves home and must make its own way. Your manuscript has a mission to do, independent of your "parenting" or vision, and its refining may require that you take a good hard look at yourself. A poem, I think, is as close as one can come to a photograph of one's psyche and soma. In it, one can see every flaw or banality of character—self-pity, self-indulgence, self-protectiveness—as well as every virtue. Thus, one cannot change one's style without changing the psyche first. This is what so many workshop teachers do not realize, that certain choices are driven by something quite deep. Change must occur on a deeper level than the technical.

Riffing off of Franz Kafka, the French philosopher Hélène Cixous elaborates:

> To deal and to receive the axe's blow, to look straight at the face of God, *which is none other than my own face,* but seen naked, the face of my soul. The face of "God" is the unveiling, the staggering vision of the construction we are, the tiny and great lies, the small untruths we must have incessantly woven to be able

> to prepare our brothers' dinner and cook for our children.[5]

If that statement doesn't scare you away from the arduous nature of the mythopoetic journey, then you may be qualified to hone your skills into an axe that can break up the frozen sea of our humanity.

I don't know who it was who said that you have to "finish" your manuscript three times before it is finally finished. Someone did, I assure you, and I agree. It's not over until the Fat Lady sings. A manuscript is a living thing, and if it isn't evolving, changing over time, then it's not living. Your draft of two years ago should be different than your current version, as different as a twelve-year-old is from a fourteen-year-old. Sometimes this is a matter of great waiting. Drafting continues from the first draft right up to when the manuscript is sent to the printer, and sometimes even after the book has come out. Unfortunately, we all come equipped with egos as part of our standard package, and so the workshop loses some of its real purpose because people want to bring in their prize poem and wow their classmates, but the best participant is one who can bring something in that they really want help with, something that hasn't yet hardened into its final form. This ability to revise is a skill that has to be learned and develops over time, but it is *the* most critical skill one can have in one's quiver. Your manuscript will go through stages of chaos and come into focus.

Making the *Mirepoix*

I like to think of the manuscript title, the first poem, and last poem as the *mirepoix* of a manuscript (the onions, red bell peppers, and celery, what the Cajuns call the "holy trinity" of their cuisine). They should create a trinity when read together. Do the title, the first poem, and the last poem work together? Do the first lines and last lines of the manuscript complete or echo one another? The effect should be one of an ouroboros, the tail-in-mouth of a serpent, a combination that creates a vortex of energy into which a reader is then swept and carried into the body of the work.

The first and last poem of a manuscript (and of every section, should you choose to divide your book) ought to be what Lucie Brock-Broido called a "mother-wicked keeper" (MWK). In an ideal world, the first three poems of a manuscript ought to be mother-wicked keepers, and when read together they ought to sound the tonalities of the entire manuscript. These are the Barry Bonds of the manuscript. Place your best poem at the top of the order. (I have known poets who wrote one great poem and put it first in a manuscript and made very successful careers out of this one placement.) You want to swing for the fences from the get-go, not get started on page seventeen. This is the number-one tactical error I see poets make; their manuscript takes a great deal of time to get started. They'll say something like: "But I won an award for this poem, and the judge cited this poem out of the group in particular," or "I identify with the frog in this poem," or "This is what was happening to me on 9/11," their rationale for beginning the manuscript with a poem that is not a mother-wicked keeper overriding the zeitgeist of the created whole entirely. "What does it have to do with your title?" I find myself asking. "This other poem makes a connection with the title from the get-go."

Another client of mine has clumped certain poems with the same theme together. They dampen each other rather than creating a harmonic resonance. Strung back to back, they compete and cancel one another out instead of creating a harmonic resonance. Once separated, they chime, aspect each other favorably. With a few changes in order, the very same manuscript with the very same poems begins to reach the finals and eventually wins a major publication prize. Order matters.

Mot-clés and Mythopoeia

In fact, because lyric poets don't generally write from a totally conscious place, not every poet is aware of what their leitmotifs are or why. In fact, it can be *dangerous* to let the right hand know what the left hand is doing or allow the superego to have too much control over the process. Carl Jung reminds us that, "In all chaos there is a cosmos, in all disorder a secret order."[6] So, too, the words "whole" and "heal" come from the same root, the same derivation.[7] Perhaps the manuscript is not yet "whole," "finished," or ready to go out into the world until it has healed something quite deep in the writer or worked something to its resolution. For Jungians, psychology means the study of and knowledge of the journey of the soul on Earth and across all perceivable worlds. The words "healing" and "whole" are related. Jung felt that the journey toward wholeness is an engagement with the mythopoetic imagination, deeming the spirit of the age as an invitation to lose our souls. According to Jung, without this half we were only half human. Jung held that fantasy had been devalued in our present age and was the means by which the soul was united with its other half.[8] We as poets are good at this kind of thing.

To practice a true psychology and a true poetry, then, we'd seek meaning in our lives through all our episodic sagas. We would define them not so much as "the good, the bad, and the downright ugly" so to speak, but rather as descents, ascents, ever seeking creative expression, mending, and meaning in more than one world—from the down-to-earth aspects, but also from what Clarissa Pinkola Estés calls "the aerial view" that sees in the ways of spirit and soul, not only ego alone. Thus, from those overviews, many episodes in life want to be art and artful, rather than only dead and deadly.

But how does one spot these I-beams of meaning, these leitmotifs? The second organizing factor in a manuscript are the *mot-clés* or keywords and images that repeat. These create a subliminal knitting together of an entire manuscript. Go through and note what these words are. You may be surprised at what you discover by doing so. When organizing the manuscript, you will want to thread these words in a way that creates a subliminal chime. When given a group of poems to order into a manuscript, I'll map these *mot-clés* and use them to arrange the manuscript. Think leitmotifs rather than subject matter here.

Momentum

Don't keep your B+ lines or your B+ poems. Throw them out.

I can't tell you how many manuscripts are stillborn because the author can't see it newly and can't see that certain elements of it are now outgrown and need to be jettisoned, let go. That first section of initiation poems, that long preamble until the manuscript begins, can take a writer years to see before letting it go. The screeners never got to read your manuscript because it started on page eighteen.

There is a vortex of energy in a poem or a manuscript. It's what I call placing the poem on the train tracks with the train coming. And there are also predilections that can block that vortex or slow the energy down. The art of poetry is difficult because we're making very subtle adjustments. We take out an adjective, but it ruins the rhythm to do so, and the adjective is superfluous on one level but does *some* work, a little bit, just enough to vampire the poem's energies, and so we are looking for all the word-horses of logo-, melo-, and phanopoeia to pull the troika of the poem across the frozen tundra of the page as efficiently as possible, keeping ahead of the wolves. The wolves are starving, so in order for the poem to survive we must be willing to let go of the heavy freight—that beautiful, faithless word and our attraction to it—and dump it heartlessly over the side. Think of it as practicing the end of codependence on the page. You can't afford these behaviors any longer. Anything can work, but know your predilections, your excesses. The verb is still the workhorse of the sentence, not the adjective. You may have to throw one or two over the side, especially those Latinate abstractions. (Don't get me wrong. I love a Latinate abstraction, but it's like using saffron in a recipe. A little goes a long way. If you love alliteration, consider less frontal forms than "Peter Piper picked . . ." Consider the interlocking consonance of internal chimes, as in the words "milk" and "lilac.") It has to be win-win all the way. Something may have to be dumped.

In his monumental essay "Quickness," Italo Calvino speaks of a proximity to death, a quickness, that makes a great poem come alive. He uses an example from an essay by English writer Thomas de Quincy's "Confessions of an Opium Eater" (1821). In a section called "The Vision of Sudden Death," De Quincy describes a night journey on a box of an express mail coach with a gigantic coachman who is fast asleep. The technical perfection of the vehicle, and the transformation of the driver into a blind inanimate object, puts the traveler at the mercy of the mechanical inexorability and momentum of a machine.[9]

Calvino attributes the power of poetic style as due in large part to rapidity, quoting Giacomo Leopardi: "The power of poetic style, which is largely the same thing as rapidity, is pleasing for these effects alone and consists in nothing else. The excitement of simultaneous ideas may arise either from each isolated word, whether literal or metaphorical, from their arrangement, from the turn of a phrase, or even from the suppression of other words and phrases."[10]

Maintain Altitude

Once you've written a line that is as superb as "About suffering they were never wrong,/ The Old Masters,"[11] there's no going back. You must maintain that altitude. One can read for a very long time and not encounter a line that is as superb as that. A great many poems in American poetry find a cruising altitude that's not, shall we say, especially dazzling, but the poem finds a way into our consciousness, a niche or a hook, and maintains cruising altitude. These poets may even enjoy a great deal of success by capturing the zeitgeist of our modernity. So, I would say, it is not I whom you have to please. It is you, yourself, who have upped the ante, and now you find yourself stuck in a favored birch tree like a young porcupine who doesn't know how to get out of the situation. You write great beginnings, but can never pin the ending. What now? Rest. Reload. Revise a thousand times. I speak as one who has spent a lot of time stuck in that tree. Genius is patience.

Like that porcupine, you, the poet, ultimately have to figure out the poem's and manuscript's best strategy for survival, and address your preferences and decide whether these mechanisms are really working for the poem or are making travel more difficult. Does your manuscript sag in the middle like an old mattress? A string of short poems can bring down the energy. Of course, ask your friends to read your manuscript-in-progress. Notice the cues. If they tell you that it was really great, but they had to put it down and head to the kitchen for a snack, take that as a hint that there's something blocking the manuscript's vortex of energy. I call this the "sandwich cue." Your friends all know your greatest flaw, but no one is going to just come right up and tell you that you're a one-trick pony or that you're didactic or that your poems are insufferably dry and academic. They're going to go make themselves a sandwich. Only a good teacher or editor is going to risk putting his or her head inside the lion's mouth to extract that infected tooth. Most of us have to figure it out for ourselves. We stink to high heaven. Maybe it's time to change your socks.

Someone with experience can save you a lot of wasted energy, but ultimately, in order to maximize the energetic vortex in a poem or a manuscript, one has to consider that lightening up for a great poem is like the weighing of a soul and ideally it is as light as a feather.

Neatness Counts

Your presentation needs to look professional. Read the guidelines. If the guidelines stipulate that the manuscript should be in 12-point Times New Roman font, that there ought not be any acknowledgments page, that no more than one poem per page should appear in the manuscript unless part of a cycle of poems, and the competition would like the name of the manuscript to appear in the top right corner of every page in the header and for the margins to be one inch from the top, then you had better adhere to the guidelines or expect to be rejected. Max Perkins is dead. The copy must be impeccable. Therefore, if you can't punctuate and know you can't, hire a proofreader. (Yes, we all make mistakes, but don't expect a benefit of a doubt. The winning manuscript has been through the mill.)

Things that tip off the screener that you're not ready for prime time and are still an amateur include an excessive use of epigraphs, dedications, asterisks accompanied by footnotes (save these for the notes at the end of the collection, if you wish), too many sections (unless brilliantly conceived), curlicue fonts, typos, confusing line breaks, using the center tab to justify the lines down the middle of the page, and excessive use of section titles. Some publishers have idiosyncratic prejudices against poems about children, pets, particular words, and other topics they consider unredeemable sentimentia.[12] Again, anything *can* work.

Other Considerations

Network. Get to know as many people as possible. Most competitions have rules against knowing the judge, but before your manuscript gets to the judge, it is going to have to go through a screener who can be your very best friend. Attend a conference or two. At the very least you will make friends for life with some of the other participants, and you will need them to endure the lonely hours and the rejections. (Don't lose heart. I have never received a rejection that wasn't surpassed by a better outcome. Never.)

Choose what you want in a publisher (distribution, a pretty cover design, that your book be kept in print). Cast a wide net. You can't possibly set your hopes on winning the Berkshire Prize, but you'd be surprised at how many poets send their manuscripts to only one or two contests a year. Cut down on that drawer time. Establish a routine around submissions. A plethora of poets suffer from Emily Dickinson syndrome and live under a very populous rock in the forest. If they'd only spend half the time submitting their work that they do kvetching about rejection on social media, they'd get somewhere. If you get rejected, aim higher, not lower. You're apt to encounter a better judge of poetry in a well-established editor who has been around the block.

Don't second-guess your judge. Sometimes when you least expect it, a judge could choose someone who no one would ever expect.

Don't pull your punches. If your manuscript is about losing all your friends during the AIDS pandemic, don't end on, "Our house is a very fine house with two cats in the yard."[13]

Polarize your opposites. "All happy families are alike," wrote Tolstoy, but writing about the unhappy one may have more piquancy. An entire manuscript of spiritual poems may need something to ground it.

Risk emotion. Galway Kinnell once told me, "A poem can be technically perfect, but if it lacks emotion, then it is a failed poem." I don't know whether this problem is a vestige of or residue from T. S. Eliot's "Tradition and the Individual Talent," now 101 years old, insisting that poetry should eschew emotion altogether, but in order to become the whole package, you must risk falling in the well of your own bathos. People may stare at you as though you came to your poetry workshop naked. You need to be willing to fall in the well, make a fool of yourself, brush yourself off, and then jump in the well again. There's no way to create that kind of deeply layered and nuanced piece of writing with the superego alone.

Make an arc. Poems need to converse with one another in a manuscript. If you have three poems about leprechauns, consider spacing them out and giving them breathing space. How many books have you read where the author has their neat little section about the death of a parent? Consider using them as supporting structures or I-beams that will support an arc if spaced throughout a manuscript.

Make rain. Paul Valery stated that "For a poet, it is never a matter of saying, "it is raining.' It is a matter of making rain."[14] We all recognize the difference between a poem that declares "it is raining" and a poem that makes rain. You may have to check your penchant for preachment and wrapping things up neatly with the bow. This single factor separates good writers from the greats.

The deep emotion, the sensitivity to language, the pith of aphorism, the irony, the music that lifts the entire piece up, the startling image, the violence or beauty of the elements, the lightness, the *sprezzatura*, the élan, the courtier's finesse, a vortex of energy that is a combination of resistance and forward movement, the polarization of opposites, the gorgeousness of aria, learning to play the sounds of language like a great pianist—the elements that constitute great writing sifted through all the layers of humanity—all take time. Remember the greatness of theater when Nora first comes onto the stage and then finally leaves Torvald in the final act in *A Doll's House*. Your manuscript should create that kind of frisson. Write the poems of a human being who knows that his or her time on this planet is limited—because it is. Walk out past the city limits of life as you have known it or believed it was, experience a paradigm shift—you, a refugee in your own country, in your own skin. Poetry is the efflorescence of human consciousness and the intelligence of one's own soul. The survival of our species depends upon the insights contained in a great book of poetry—yours.

Endnotes

1 Fred Fisher (composer), Sophie Tucker (vocalist), "Fifty Million Frenchmen Can't Be Wrong," 1927.

2 Voltaire (1764), "Art dramatique," *Dictionnaire philosophique* (in French), published in 1878: "C'est bien ici qu'on peut dire: Il meglio è l'inimico del bene."

3 Robert Herrick, "Upon Julia's Clothes," *Hesperides* (1648).

4 Franz Kafka, *Letters to Friends, Family, and Editors,* trans. Richard and Clara Winston (New York: Shocken, 1978), 16.

5 Hélène Cixous, *Three Steps on the Ladder of Writing,* trans. Sarah Cornell and Susan Sellers (New York: Columbia University Press, 1993), 63.

6 C. G. Jung, *The Archetypes and the Collective Unconscious* (*Collected Works of C. G. Jung*, Volume 9, Part 1) (Princeton, NJ: Princeton University Press, 1981), 32.

7 "The Proto-Germanic word 'khailaz,' which means 'to make whole,' is the root of both 'to heal' and the closely related word 'health.'" Vocabulary.com, https://www.vocabulary.com/dictionary/heal.

8 Lance Owens, "The Hermeneutics of Vision: C. G. Jung and Liber Novus," Gnosis.org, 2010, http://gnosis.org/Lance-Owens.html.

9 Italo Calvino, "Quickness," *Six Memos for the Next Millenium* (London: Penguin Group, 2009), 40.

10 Giacomo Leopardi, "Ziabaldone di pensieri," quoted in Italo Calvino, "Quickness," ibid., 42.

11 W. H. Auden, "Musée des Beaux Arts."

12 Liam Rector coined the term "sentimentia" and defined it as "sentiment commingled with dementia."

13 Graham Nash, "Our House."

14 Paul Valéry, "Mes Theatres" (1942), in *Œuvres 1* (Paris: Gallimard, La Pleiade, 1971), 403.

An Exercise for Sequencing Full-Length Poetry Manuscripts: Three Different Sequencing Techniques

Jeffrey Levine

These revision exercises are part of our curriculum at the Tupelo Press Manuscript Conference Series, where working writers from around the world have come to perfect their poetry collections at the levels of line, structure, and sequencing.

Like a satisfying poem, a well-structured collection has an arc, a shape that resembles narrative or story.

With that said, we tend to forget that many stories are possible from the same set of facts, and many potential sequences are contained within a single group of poems. Your task will be to uncover at least three possible stories that your collection can tell.

First, print out a single section of your manuscript. If your manuscript doesn't have sections, simply print out the first fifteen poems. Then sequence them in the following ways:

- **Creating a narrative arc:** Look closely at the last lines and titles/openings of each poem. Place them in the order that seems most natural when considering the transition between the ending of one poem and the beginning of the next.
- **Creating tension:** Place your poems in an order that juxtaposes vastly different aspects of your voice and your aesthetic. This can mean thematic shifts, shifts in tone, shifts in form, shifts in voice or the type of speaker we are presented with, or all of the above.

- **Allowing formal shifts to become content:** Start with a poem that seems like a natural opening for that sequence. Then, follow it up with a formal shift, one that is meaningful when considered after the opening poem. For example, starting with a poem in couplets, then presenting something fractured, fragmented, can read as a powerful commentary on the narrative. This is just one possibility, and you'll need to consider how the different forms you're working with can illuminate the story your poems are telling.

As you work, keep in mind these questions: Which of these techniques are you underutilizing? Are there moments where you could vary your strategy when it comes to sequencing the poems, allowing for greater surprise, variation, and tension?

A Follow-Up Assignment for Sequencing Full-Length Poetry Manuscripts: Transitions

You should have three differently sequenced versions of your manuscript, using three different sequencing techniques. For this exercise, you will choose your favorite pairings of individual poems from each different version of your manuscript. From each different sequencing, you will pull out the pairs of poems you think transition most effectively. It is fine if the poem pairs you select transition in completely different ways.

Set these pairings of individual poems aside, clearly marking which poems go with which. Once you have a fair amount of poem pairs, you will begin building a structure from the ground up, selecting other poems that would complement each pairing.

Revision Exercise: Title Bank

As you revise, the narrative arc may shift, and some titles may no longer suit individual poems, sections of the manuscript, or the work as a whole. In order to prepare for this stage of the revision process, it's often wise to create a "title bank," a list of phrases, lines, and pieces of language that call out to you as possible titles for a finished work.

Your first task will be to mine your manuscript, creating a Word document of phrases from your own poems that contain worlds. Once you've exhausted your own manuscript, move on to a literary text that was important to the creation of your own book. Choose phrases from that literary text that are similar to your own voice in tone and style, and also language that's much different. Then move on to at least one nonliterary text, culling pieces of language that could strike sparks against one of your poems.

Bear in mind that titles can do many different types of work in a poem or sequence: providing context for the poem, complicating the poem, creating tension with the poem itself, describing its narrative arc, instructing the reader as to how to engage with, and imagine with, that poem, teaching us how to read form or formal shifts, and so on. You'll want to cull language that could serve each of these purposes in relation to your work.

As you sequence your manuscript, you will discover that titles can be powerful bridges between individual poems. The title bank offers an invaluable resource as you create continuity and structure on the level of the book.

Revision Exercise: The Shadow Story

In a recent craft essay that appeared in the *Black Warrior Review*, Jennifer Cheng notes that "every story has a shadow story." The "shadow story" haunts the narrative proper, following the arc of the collection with the utmost fidelity, but never making itself fully known. (For more on the shadow story see the essay by Kristina Marie Darling, "'Almost Everyone Was Mistaken': On Secrets, Light, and the Lyric Imagination," pp. XXX above.)

When considering a poetry manuscript as a whole, this shadow story can be incredibly meaningful, even more so than what is plainly stated in the poems.

As you revise, make a list of all the elements of plot and narrative we are given in your sequence. Then consider the following questions:

- What is left unsaid in the larger arc of your collection, and why?
- What is the story of that silence?
- What do these silences reveal about the speaker(s) of your poems and their emotional/psychic landscapes?
- Where in the manuscript could you potentially exercise greater restraint, allowing the silence to speak?

Conclusion

As noted by many of the essays in this book, achieving a meaningful and effective sequence of poems in your manuscript is critical to its success. Take the time to do the exercises suggested here, and your attention and work will be rewarded.

Contest Manuscripts: Behind the Scenes at Tupelo Press

Jeffrey Levine

> The doorkeeper's feet are seven armlengths long
> five oxhides for his sandals
> ten shoemakers worked on them
>
> —Fragment of Sappho (110) translated by Anne Carson (*If Not, Winter*, Knopf, 2002)

Why are these lines, fragments of lines—all that remain legible on a papyrus, a song of Sappho—sitting here atop this short piece on what happens to the contest manuscripts submitted to Tupelo Press?

Those three truncated lines of Sappho become indelible in a single reading. They offer up a certain transparency (piercing), a certain reverberation (overtones, echoes, resonance), a certain immediate apprehending of what, for want of a better, more specific word, let's call "beauty." These fragments—a lyric—not only suggest but also handle so authoritatively what Gregory Orr in his brilliant book *Poetry as Survival* (University of Georgia Press, 2002) calls "the flux and chaos of feeling." What do I mean by "handle"? Grasp, seize, touch, carry, manage, deal with, be responsible for, manipulate, control.

A manuscript is itself both a handle and a threshold. It occupies a liminal state in that exotic, rarefied, arcane culture constituted by the writers and potential publishers of poetry. Which is to say that each submitted manuscript exists in a transitional state, offering itself up for a kind of initiation ceremony in which, as with other ceremonies that mark transitional states (marriages, funerals, bar mitzvahs, crownings, beheadings, carving the Thanksgiving turkey), ordinary social rules are suspended, and the submitted pages are asking to undergo a profound change in identity.

The ritual reading process guides each of these manuscripts through this symbolic "space" of potential transformation. At the threshold, where manuscripts are read, as Gregory Orr might say, "linguistic, imaginative, and emotional energies are vastly heightened."

Every manuscript is an offering, each reading a ceremony. This, then, is how I think of the process of reading manuscripts here at Tupelo Press. Even if there is no trumpet fanfare, no gathering of the court, no large, loyal dog at my side (there is a large, not-so-loyal cat), no glass of sherry in my hand, there is something fully ceremonial about the process.

Reading each manuscript is an event, informed by the knowledge that every submission constitutes someone's lifework, and that each is the product of months or years of solitary hours, and the manuscript is freighted with this work, this history, the workings of the imagination, the repeated gathering of inner forces, the summoning of the unconscious and countless invocations of the muse. The weight of time itself collects in those pages, just as time has collected in the papyri of Sappho, enhancing each fragment by the physical diminishment of the very page on which it appears.

You may remember that Jorge Luis Borges called the universe a book, and said that he imagined paradise "in the shape of a library" ("Poema de los Dones," in *El Hacedor*, Emecé, 1960). Our job—the job of every publisher—is to populate those libraries, the physical artifacts that survive the generations.

For example, each winter here at the Tupelo loft in the NORAD Mill in North Adams, Massachusetts, at the confluence of Mount Greylock, Mount Prospect, Mount Pine Cobble, and Mount Williams, we read for the Dorset Prize, a competition open to poets writing in English anywhere in the world. We get submissions, both online and hard copy, from Nepal, India, New Zealand, France, Australia, Canada, Germany, Ireland, England, Scotland, Russia, Israel, Japan, China, Lebanon, Greece, Turkey, Italy, Mexico, Uruguay, Spain, and just about everywhere else on the globe. Also, of course, and mainly, from within the United States. There is no way in which this kind of diversity is not thrilling.

To start the process, each manuscript is "logged in," which means it's entered into our database, the cover pages, bios, cover letters, and all other identifying materials detached and filed, and as well the acknowledgment pages, those too, removed and filed. The manuscripts are numbered consecutively, as received, then put in stacks to be read.

What happens to those manuscripts, exactly?

Who reads them? Kristina Marie Darling, our Editor-in-Chief does, as I do, with the assistance of several of the most experienced and widely published poets in the land. We don't use interns to screen submissions. We generally receive about 1,200–1,500 submissions for each of our poetry prizes and, as well, for our July–August open reading period. Each time, it takes two or three months of steady reading to complete the task.

Is our aesthetic a knowable thing? Well, yes, of course it is. Any poet who reads, closely and attentively, any five books we've published in the last three years will know what we like, or at least, have a useful sense of the parameters of our tastes.

Does it matter when the manuscripts come in, i.e., closer to the start or closer to the end of a contest period? No, not at all. It's only the work itself that matters.

Does it matter whether manuscripts are submitted in hard copy or electronically? No, not at all, though these days, almost all arrive electronically through Submittable, our submissions management platform.

Do cover letters count? No, not for contests. We don't read them. Or anyway, not until after we've sent a dozen or so finalists off to our judge. Then, because we're curious, once a contest is over Kristina and I may read the cover letters. But in contest situations, cover letters are detached and filed. (This is not the case, however, during our July–August open reading period. I love reading cover letters, and as this open reading period is not a contest and not anonymous, I also crave the opportunity to have a sense of the person behind the poems.)

Why do we ask for an acknowledgments page if we don't look at it? Excellent question. There are three reasons:

- Because we do look at them after the contest is over.
- Because we're curious (see above) about where our submitters are publishing, and what those published poems say about the editorial aesthetic at various literary journals and magazines.
- Because sometimes, not so rarely, actually, we take for publication a manuscript or two out of the contest stacks just because it appeals to us, and when we do, we like to know where those poems have been, and that the poet has been doing the hard and essential work of building a readership for their work.

What happens during the actual reading process? We read closely. If I get that sensation I described above, something similar to the feeling I get from reading those lines of Sappho: i.e., that there's something indelible going on, that there's an authority in the voice, that real ideas reside in the poems, that the poet is in full control of the craft of writing poetry, that there are overtones, echoes, resonance in the lines, that I'm finding the work memorable, that I'm making discoveries because the poet has made discoveries, well then, in however many pages it takes to convince myself that what's found there is something special, I mark that manuscript in some runic way and put it aside for further reading.

How far will we read into a manuscript before deciding whether or not it makes the next round? It could be twenty pages. Or thirty. Enough to know that we're in the hands of an exciting imagination.

What separates the manuscripts that get marked for further reading from the ones that do not? Craft. Ideas. Resonance. Control. Authority of voice. Whether or not the work is memorable. And more often than you might think, the consistency of the work across the manuscript. Many, if not most manuscripts have several fabulous poems. Few manuscripts are made entirely of fabulous poems. Which is just one reason why I encourage submitters to enter manuscripts of around 52 to 64 pages. I would venture to say that in every contest submission period there are always 200 or 300 manuscripts by poets to be reckoned with.

What about titles? Good titles help. Bad titles don't help. If I get a batch of otherwise great manuscripts with awful titles, I might ask the judge to ignore the titles, but I'm sure that this direction results in raised eyebrows.

What's the best preparation for writing and submitting a manuscript? Read everything. Read some more. Read systematically. Write many, many craft annotations of poems. When you read, ask yourself, "What exactly is going on in that poem with respect to two or three elements of craft?" Read voraciously in other disciplines. Memorize a good dozen poems so that you absorb them. At least one William Carlos Williams, at least one Wallace Stevens, some Emily Dickinson, at least one Shakespeare, and so on. Memorize a few contemporary poems that speak to you. Figure them out. Do this work. There is no substitute for it.

What about order? What about arc? Normally we don't get to those considerations until later rounds, meaning, when we've gotten to about 100 surviving manuscripts (about four rounds into the reading process), then we start to consider closely questions of order, questions of internal coherence, questions of overall strategy.

How do we get from 100 manuscripts to twelve finalists and about twenty semifinalists? We read them over and over and over again. We discuss. We argue. We look at order. We look at strategy. We think about the project that motors the manuscript. Then we put the book down and let it percolate. See what draws us back. It's that memorable quality at work again. We look for collections of poetry that we can't live without. That doesn't mean there aren't poems—often many poems—in other manuscripts that we can't live without. But there's a vital difference between manuscripts that boast many memorable poems, and a fully memorable, fully deserving manuscript.

Is the reading process really anonymous? Yes, it really is anonymous. An astute reader of our lists will notice that more than half of the previous winners of our various poetry prizes have been first books. I love that this happens. You might remember earlier that I said it's the work that matters. And only the work that matters. I still mean it.

How does it happen that a manuscript that was a semifinalist one year doesn't make the cut the next year? Yes, that sometimes happens. Because we're always reading each manuscript in context with all the other entries. Because we're human, and because our tastes and appetites change. Some years we find ourselves loving the more experimental work. Other years we may find ourselves drawn to more traditional approaches. But, as anyone who has spent some time with Tupelo's lists will attest, our tastes are quite diverse, so long as it's fabulous, transcendent, life-altering work.

If my manuscript doesn't make the cut, is there any point in resubmitting? Good question. Few manuscripts have won our contests on the first try; several of our winning authors have submitted many times. The idea is to create and submit a "competitive manuscript." But that said, rather than simply resubmitting a manuscript, we recommend approaching your work with close attention to revision, to reentering and reimagining the work, to finding those discoveries that a poem will yield up over time to the most patient writer. At the very least, you're getting an intensely careful and attentive reading of your work.

What steps does Tupelo Press take to ensure that our contest judges are fair? We're as rigorous as can be about this. You can find our ethical doctrine on our website. We find that judges will bend over backward to be fair and ethical. The work of judging a poetry contest is hard, exciting, and rewarding, and I've never encountered a judge of any one of our contests who wasn't in it for the discoveries to be made.

How do I get to have one of those manuscripts that's chosen for publication even though it didn't win your contest? Answer: Fill your work with that "flux and chaos of feeling" that Greg Orr writes about, and make us have to come back to it over and over and over again.

Do we sometimes miss the boat on great work? You bet. We have many times passed on manuscripts that we wish we'd taken.

Do other independent literary presses have identical processes? No. Each press has its own process, just as each has its own aesthetic. I tend to think that each one of us is alike in the way that Tom Lux puts it (about writing poetry) in his ars poetica, "An Horatian Notion": *We do the thing because we love the thing.*

Contributor Biographies

Cassandra Cleghorn

Cassandra Cleghorn was born in upstate New York, raised in southern California, and studied Greek at the University of California, Santa Cruz and American Studies at Yale University. Her first book, *Four Weathercocks,* was published by Marick Press in 2016. Her poems have been published in many journals including *Paris Review, New Orleans Review, Yale Review, Southwest Review, Narrative, The Common,* and *Poetry International.* She lives in northwestern Massachusetts where she teaches at Williams College and serves as Poetry Editor of Tupelo Press.

Kristina Marie Darling

Kristina Marie Darling is the author of over thirty volumes of poetry, essays, and fiction. An expert consultant with the United States Fulbright Commission and a twice-awarded Fulbright Scholar, Dr. Darling's work has also been recognized with three residencies at Yaddo, where she has held the Martha Walsh Pulver Residency for a Poet and the Howard Moss Residency in Poetry, a 2024 Villa Lena Foundation Fellowship, eleven juried residencies at the American Academy in Rome, and a nomination for the Distinguished Visitor Fellowship at the American Academy in Berlin. She has held academic appointments at Universidade do Porto, the European Law and Governance School, the Amsterdam School for Cultural Analysis, the American Research Center in Sofia, and the Leysin American School in Switzerland. A prolific public speaker with the Ovation Agency, Dr. Darling has also lectured at Yale University, the American University in Rome, Stanford University, Columbia University in the City of New York, the New School, the University of Cyprus, the *Los Angeles Review of Books* Publishing Workshop, Cedar Crest College's Pan-European MFA

Program, and Webster University's Geneva, Switzerland, campus, where she leads a biannual writing workshop for diplomats. Additionally, Dr. Darling has served on fellowship juries for the United States Fulbright Commission, the Corporation of Yaddo, the Millay Colony for the Arts, the Kimmel Harding Nelson Center for the Arts, the Helene Wurlitzer Foundation, and many other awards in the United States and abroad. Born and raised in the American Midwest, she now divides her time between Greece, Spain, and the Amalfi Coast.

Kathy Fagan

Kathy Fagan's fifth poetry collection, *Sycamore* (Milkweed, 2017), was a finalist for the 2018 Kingsley Tufts Award. Her new book with Milkweed will be published in Autumn 2022. Fagan's work has appeared in venues such as *The New York Times Sunday Magazine, Poetry, The Nation, The New Republic, Kenyon Review, The Academy of American Poets Poem-A-Day* and *Best American Poetry.* The recipient of grants from the Ingram Merrill Foundation, the Ohio Arts Council and the NEA, Fagan is co-founder of the MFA Program at The Ohio State University where she teaches poetry and co-edits the Wheeler Poetry Prize Book Series for *The Journal* and OSU Press.

Katie Farris

Katie Farris's work has been commissioned by MoMA and appears in *American Poetry Review, Granta, McSweeneys, The Nation*, and *Poetry*. She is the author of *boysgirls* (Tupelo Pess) and a co-editor of *Gossip and Metaphysics: Russian Modernist Poetry and Prose* (Tupelo Press). Her chapbook *A Net to Catch My Body in its Weaving,* won the 2020 Chad Walsh Poetry Award from *Beloit Poetry Journal*. Her next book of poetry, *Standing in the Forest of Being Alive,* was published by Alice James Books in 2023.

Lise Goett

Lise Goett's most recent book, *Leprosarium* (Tupelo Press, 2018), was a selection in the 2015 July Open Reading Period of Tupelo Press and the 2012 winner of the Robert H. Winner Memorial Award in Poetry from the Poetry Society of America for best manuscript-in-progress by a poet over forty. Her other awards include *The Paris Review* Discovery Award, the *Palette* Spotlight Award, The Pen Southwest Book Award in Poetry, the Capricorn Prize from the West Side Y, the James D. Phelan Award from the San Francisco Foundation, and The Barnard New Women Poets Prize for her first poetry collection, *Waiting for the Paraclete* (Beacon, 2002), as well as postgraduate fellowships from The Milton Center and the Creative Writing Institute at the University of Wisconsin-Madison. Her poetry has appeared in numerous journals, including *The Paris Review, Ploughshares, Lana Turner, Image, Mandorla*, and the Antioch Review. She is a core faculty member at the Tupelo Writers Conference in Truchas, New Mexico and has shepherded dozens of private clients to manuscript-publication success through her online editing services and generative workshops.

Ilya Kaminsky

Ilya Kaminsky is the author *of Dancing in Odessa* (Tupelo Press) and *Deaf Republic* (Graywolf Press). He has edited or translated several other books with Tupelo Press, including *God in the House: Poets Talk About God, This Lamentable City: Poems of Polina Barskova*, and *Gossip and Metaphysics: Russian Modernist Poems and Prose*. His work has received The Los Angeles Times Book Award and Guggenheim Fellowship and he was a finalist for the National Book Award and National Book Critics Circle Award.

Jeffrey Levine

Jeffrey Levine is the author of four books of poetry: *At the Kinnegad Home for the Bewildered* (Salmon Press February 2019), *Rumor of Cortez*, nominated for a 2006 *Los Angeles Times* Literary Award in Poetry, *Mortal, Everlasting*, which won the 2002 Transcontinental Poetry Prize, and *The After Party*, is coming from Salmon Press in 2026. He is also the translator of Pablo Neruda's *Canto General, Song of the Americas.* His many poetry prizes include the Larry Levis Prize from the *Missouri Review*, the James Hearst Poetry Prize from *North American Review*, the *Mississippi Review* Poetry Prize, the *Ekphrasis* Poetry Prize, and the *American Literary Review* poetry prize. His poems have garnered twenty-three Pushcart nominations. A graduate of the Warren Wilson MFA Program for Writers, Levine is founder, Artistic Director, and Publisher of Tupelo Press, an award-winning independent literary press located in the historic NORAD Mill in the Berkshire Mountains of Western Massachusetts.